LINCOLN
As He Really Was

LINCOLN
As He Really Was

Dr. Charles T. Pace

Foreword by
Dr. Thomas J. DiLorenzo

SHOTWELL PUBLISHING
COLUMBIA, SOUTH CAROLINA

LINCOLN AS HE REALLY WAS
Copyright © 2018 by Charles T. Pace

ALL RIGHTS RESERVED. No part of this publication may be reproduced, distributed, or transmitted in any form or by any means, including photocopying, recording, or other electronic or mechanical methods, or by any information storage and retrieval system without the prior written permission of the publisher, except in the case of very brief quotations embodied in critical reviews and certain other non-commercial uses permitted by copyright law.

Produced in the Republic of South Carolina by

SHOTWELL PUBLISHING, LLC
Post Office Box 2592
Columbia, South Carolina 29202

www.ShotwellPublishing.com

Cover Image: Abraham Lincoln, 1863. Photograph by Lewis Emory Walker. Courtesy Library of Congress.
Cover Design: Hazel's Dream / Boo Jackson TCB

ISBN-13: 978-1947660151
ISBN-10: 1947660152

10 9 8 7 6 5 4 3 2 1

Contents

Foreword vii
Apologia xv
Introduction: The Lincoln Legend 1
Origins 11
New Salem 21
A Henry Clay Man 29
First Rung on the Ladder 37
"Emancipating Slaves" 49
Springfield: A Bigger Stage 57
Depression 65
Backing Down 73
A Thirst for Distinction 83
A One-Term Congressman 93
Obstructive But Unnoticed 103
Perfecting the Style 111
Storm Watch 121
Cautiously Republican 131
Coming Out 139
Riding the Rising Tide 149
The Biggest Stage of All 165
Cold in Crisis 177
Country or Party? 189
The Trap is Sprung 199
Epilogue: "Enslaving Free Men" 215
Select Bibliography 225
Index 229
About the Author 233

FOREWORD
Dr. Thomas J. DiLorenzo

DESPITE THE FACT that there are well over 10,000 books in print about Abraham Lincoln it is almost impossible for the average American — or anyone else — to know the truth about the real Lincoln. Having given hundreds of public presentations, appeared on dozens of radio talk shows (including the Rush Limbaugh Radio Show), and participated in numerous debates on the subject of Lincoln, I have learned that the average American knows nothing at all about the man except for the few slogans and platitudes that we are all taught in elementary school (and then repeated endlessly in the popular culture).

As an elementary school student in the Pennsylvania public schools I was taught that Lincoln was so honest that he once walked six miles to return a penny to a merchant who had mistakenly undercharged him. Decades later, when I debated Harry Jaffa who, like the man he called "Father Abraham," was a student of rhetoric (but not of American history), Jaffa assured the Oakland, California, audience of several hundred that Lincoln's political speeches were in fact "the words of God." (This presumably did not include his dirty jokes, for which he was famous.)

Abraham Lincoln is the only American president that has literally been deified like a Roman emperor (Like Julius Caesar, his image was the first to be placed on his country's coinage). Lincoln's deification eventually spread to the presidency, and then to the entire federal government. The Lincoln myth is thus the ideological cornerstone of the global American empire and has been for generations. As Robert Penn Warren wrote in *The*

Legacy of the Civil War, the deification of Lincoln (and of the government in general) has been used to argue that the "Civil War" left the U.S. government with "a treasury of virtue," a "plenary indulgence, for all sins past, present, and future." Consequently, American foreign policy intervention anywhere in the world is said to be always virtuous, by definition, because it is, well, American.

For more than 150 years this "treasury" of *false* virtue has been invoked to "justify" the slaughter of the Plains Indians from 1865-1898; the mass murder of some 200,000 Filipinos at the turn of the century; the imperialistic Spanish-American War; entry into Europe's war in 1918; and myriad other interventions, from Korea to Vietnam to Somalia, Lebanon, Bosnia, Grenada, Panama, Nicaragua, Yugoslavia, Haiti, Iraq, Syria, Afghanistan, and on and on. It is all a part of "our diplomacy of righteousness, with the slogan of unconditional surrender and universal spiritual rehabilitation *for others*" (emphasis added), wrote Robert Penn Warren. Professor Mel Bradford called the Lincolnian rhetoric that is the ideological basis for all this interventionism "the rhetoric of continuing revolution."

This revolutionary rhetoric is alive and well today. When Newt Gingrich authored a *Wall Street Journal* article in which he advocated the military invasion of Iran, Syria, and North Korea during the George W. Bush administration, he naturally titled the article "Lincoln and Bush," implying that such belligerence would be "Lincolnesque" and therefore should not be questioned. When the Marxist historian Eric Foner of Columbia University opposed the breakup of the Soviet Union in an October 1991 article in *The Nation* magazine he titled the article "Lincoln's Lesson." Unlike Gorbachev, he said, Lincoln would never have let the Soviet satellite states secede in peace.

The Communist Party USA used to hold "Lincoln-Lenin Day" rallies and had a giant portrait of Lincoln in its New York City offices. Even the former dictator of Pakistan, Pervez Musharref, invoked Lincoln's unconstitutional suspension of the writ of *Habeas Corpus* to "justify" martial law in *his* country. The deification of Lincoln has become a useful rhetorical tool for tyrants, militarists, and enemies of freedom everywhere.

Americans have been progressively dumbed down about Lincoln thanks to the avalanche of myths, superstitions, and propaganda produced by generations of "Lincoln scholars." It wasn't always that way, however. During his lifetime Lincoln was actually the most hated and detested of all American presidents, as documented by historian Larry Tagg in *The Unpopular Mr. Lincoln: The Story of America's Most Reviled President*. For example, on page 435 of his book Larry Tagg cites an 1864 *Harper's Weekly* article that compiled a list of terms used to describe Lincoln in the *Northern* press, including "Filthy storyteller, Ignoramus Abe, Despot, Old Scoundrel . . . Perjurer, Liar, Robber, Thief. Swindler, Braggart, Tyrant, Buffoon, Usurper, Butcher, Monster ...." The "spectacular prejudice" against Lincoln was "shocking for its cruelty, intensity, and unrelenting vigor," wrote Tagg, a native of Lincoln, Illinois.

This all changed after the assassination as the Republican Party reveled in what Tagg calls a "propaganda windfall." They would rewrite history with the help of the New England clergy in order to impose on Americans their version of what is essentially a New England theocracy composed of a government of nannies, pests, busybodies, tyrants, and money-grubbing plutocrats (known as "Yankees" by some).

New England pastors who had excoriated Lincoln for four years all of a sudden "rewrote their Easter sermons to include a new, exalted view of Lincoln as an American Moses, a leader out of slavery, a national savior who was not allowed to cross over into the Promised Land" himself. Senator James Grimes of Iowa *boasted* that the Republican Party's deification of Lincoln "has made it impossible to speak the truth about Abraham Lincoln hereafter."

Senator Grimes was right. In his 1943 book, *The Deification of Lincoln,* historian Ira D. Cardiff wrote that by then Americans were not even "interested ... in the real Lincoln. They desire a supernatural Lincoln, a Lincoln with none of the faults or frailties of the common man ... a savior, leading us to democracy and liberty — though most said readers are not interested in democracy or liberty." Moreover, said Cardiff, "a biography of Lincoln which told the truth about him would probably have great difficulty in finding a publisher."

Well, no longer. *Lincoln as He Really Was* by Charles T. Pace is a refreshingly truthful antidote to the standard Lincoln mythology. It is refreshing because it is so fact-based and well documented and devoted to historical truth. *Lincoln as He Really Was* is not your typical boring, voluminous biography filled with thousands of disconnected (and often irrelevant) facts dug up by a dozen graduate research assistants and published by a card-carrying member of the Ivy League Lincoln cult. It is the first book since Edgar Lee Masters' 1931 classic, *Lincoln the Man,* to attempt to reveal the truth about *what kind of man Abraham Lincoln really was.*

Based on voluminous research of Lincoln's actions, first and foremost, and not just his rhetoric, Pace describes how Lincoln was an expert manipulator of people; extremely lazy when it came to physical labor (contrary to the "rail splitter" legend!); was not at all well-read; and what he did read was almost exclusively books about speech-making and rhetoric, with titles such as *Lessons in Elocution.* The book confirms in spades what economist Murray N. Rothbard once said about Lincoln in an (online) essay entitled "Just War": Lincoln was a "master politician," said Rothbard, defined as one who is a masterful "liar, conniver, and manipulator." He makes any "master politician" or our time look amateurish by comparison.

Lincoln never joined a church, and both his law partner William Herndon and his wife Mary Todd said he was not a Christian. His White House assistant, Colonel Ward Lamon, called him "an infidel." His close associate Judge David Davis, whom he appointed to the Supreme Court, wrote that Lincoln "had no faith, in the Christian sense of the term." But his mother read him *Bible* stories as a child, and later in life he studied the *Bible* for *political* purposes — to use religious rhetoric to sway the masses to favour his political positions. These positions were almost exclusively the Whig economic program of protectionism, corporate welfare, and a government-run national bank to dispense subsidies to politically-connected corporations, especially his former employers, the railroad corporations. He boasted of always being a "Henry Clay Man," Clay being the leader of party of the corrupt, corporate welfare-seeking plutocracy — the Northern Whigs and then the Republicans.

Pace shows what a political animal Lincoln really was, a "zealous party man" who honed his skills, such as they were, of personally attacking his political opponents with often over-the-top ad hominem assaults, similar to how the Marxists of his day, and our day, argue(d).

None of Lincoln's family members voted for him, nor did 20 of the 23 ministers in his hometown of Springfield, Illinois. He did not even carry his own county in the 1860 election. These are the people who knew him best.

Lincoln was a master story teller, many of which were notoriously vulgar and crude. He never passed up an opportunity to make a speech, writes Pace, as he spent years honing the skills of the master politician. He could sound like an abolitionist in front of a Massachusetts audience, and the exact opposite in Southern Illinois. His speeches were always vague and his positions hard to pin down, the hallmark of a successful politician. He viewed politics as "life itself" and was intensely partisan, routinely denouncing his political opponent as "villains." He was a "born politician," writes Pace. He was, in other words, the very kind of man that George Washington, Thomas Jefferson, Patrick Henry, and James Madison warned their fellow citizens about with their admonitions about how government needed to be "bound by the chains of the Constitution" (Jefferson). "[I]t is of great importance," Madison wrote in *Federalist* 51, "to guard society against the oppression of its rulers."

Lincoln invited no family members to his wedding; chose not to attend his own father's funeral; and is said to have never had a real friend. He had a "preacher's voice" with a practiced "metaphysical tone" and was not afraid to tell outrageous lies for political purposes. For example, he insisted that the South wanted to begin enslaving poor whites and immigrants and bring slavery back to New England, where it had ended for purely economic reasons. He denied that he wanted war, or to destroy the union, or to destroy the South, and then proceeded to do every one of those things.

Lincoln as He Really Was ends with a masterful exposition of how Lincoln used all the skills of the master politician, accumulated over three decades, to incite South Carolinians into firing on Fort Sumter in order to use the incident (where no one was harmed or killed) to "justify" waging war on the South. His war cost the lives of as many as 750,000 Americans according to the latest research in order to "save the union," his professed war goal, and that of the U.S. Congress as well. Of course, in reality his war *destroyed* the *voluntary* union of states created by the founders and replaced it with a more Soviet-style, compulsory "union" held together by violence, death, mass killing, and coercion.

You, dear reader, may believe that there is something fishy about The Official History of Abraham Lincoln. Or perhaps you are incensed that you have been lied to all your life by the politically controlled/politically correct education establishment. If so, *Lincoln as He Really Was* is a must-read as a first step in your rehabilitation as an educated American citizen — or as the citizen of any other country. It will be especially helpful in allowing your children and grandchildren to have an opportunity to learn the truth about this important aspect of American history.

Thomas DiLorenzo is the author of *The Real Lincoln; Lincoln Unmasked; Hamilton's Curse;* and *The Problem with Socialism.*

APOLOGIA

MY EDUCATION IN COLLEGE was scientific — mathematics, physics, chemistry, zoology; in medical school it was the study of man's structure, his form, his gross and microscopic qualities, his function, his diseases. There not a mention was made of Lincoln — the course of study being only a steady search for scientific truth. The doctor, like the farmer, is, in his limited sphere, looking for reality. In clinical experience, both in training years and in my own practice, I saw men and women who served to the best of their ability the needs of the sick. In my mature years I finally had time to read outside my profession. I read of America's supreme figure: "Honest Abe." I learned that whatever he was, he was certainly no doctor. He lived a different life.

There were two Lincolns — the myth and the man.

Charles T. Pace
Greenville, North Carolina

Introduction:
The Lincoln Legend

History — A lie agreed upon. —Napoleon Bonaparte

THE MOST CELEBRATED, the most honoured person in all American history is Abraham Lincoln, who appears to have superseded George Washington at the summit of the national pantheon. The Lincoln image has about it the aspects of divinity. Scholars of history and politics generally make him out to be the greatest of American presidents, with Washington — the father of his country — a mere also-ran.

More books — 16,000 by recent count, with new titles popping up constantly — concern themselves with Lincoln than with any other American of note. His lean body, care-lined face, and stovepipe hat are instantly recognisable around the world. Whereas almost no one can quote a Washington speech (save, occasionally, the words from the Farewell Address concerning "the spirit of party"), schoolchildren memorize and recite at least portions of "The Gettysburg Address." The historic Ford's Theatre, where the President was assassinated in 1865, has been renovated as a venue for works "that captivate and entertain while examining political and social issues related to Lincoln's legacy." Since February 2012, the theater has been home to a Center for Education and Leadership, emphasizing "Lincoln's leadership qualities and his focus on courage, integrity, sympathy, and tolerance, ideals of equality, creativity and innovation."[1]

The shock of his assassination at the moment of military victory certainly kindled the cult of "Father Abraham," fallen martyr — just as the murder of President John F. Kennedy, a century later, would produce the only modern myth to rival Lincoln's own. He has become in some sense a brand. A luxury automobile bears his name, the $5 bill his face. All over America (though less so, conspicuously, in the South) there are Lincoln schools, Lincoln universities, Lincoln financial advisory companies, Lincoln shopping centers and property companies — all seeking in some measure to draw on Lincoln's posthumous reputation for down-home integrity. The movies long have lionized him. In 2012 alone, one film featured Lincoln himself as tracker-down of vampires, another as wartime leader and master politician — no doubt the weirdest combination of personae in all of cinema history.

Washington, D.C.'s Greek temple of a memorial to the fallen president sums up in many ways the modern view of the man — fatherly, benevolent, wise, all-seeing. From the enormous chair his statue occupies in the Lincoln Memorial, Lincoln's Olympian gaze seems to fall upon the whole country. The man is larger, it would seem, than life itself. The historian and Lincoln biographer Reinhard Luthin calls him "America's all-time favourite son."[2]

We are overdue some major adjustments of viewpoint: only in part because of the heroic Washington's decline in general esteem:

---

[1] See http://rememberinglincoln.fords.org/about-fords-theatre (Accessed 18 March 2018).
[2] Reinhard H. Luthin, *The Real Abraham Lincoln*, Prentice-Hall, 1960, xii.

from "first in war, first in peace, and first in the hearts of his countrymen" (Gen. "Light Horse Harry" Lee's encomium) to the position of runner-up in the celebrity sweepstakes. That decline is pronouncedly odd. Washington was capable, brave and honest — everything that an earlier America believed him to have been. He deserves a grade of almost perfect in establishing the new government of the United States and serving as its first president.

Lincoln "freed the slaves"? Such is the legend (further immortalized in the Stephen Spielberg movie seen all over the world in 2012 and 2013). It seems more plausible to observe that the bloody war he initiated — a war he thought, incredibly, would be short and modest in cost — brought about the end of slavery, amid the wreckage of the American republic. Meanwhile, the signal achievement of all American history — Washington's liberation of the 13 colonies from subservience to the British crown — was the deed that made possible all subsequent deeds performed by Americans in behalf of human freedom.

Possibly the Revolution was an event easy to take for granted in after years, when the founding generation had expired. Had the split with Britain been too clean for appreciation, too free of post-revolutionary turmoil and destruction? Boring, almost? Washington, large in moral perspective, as in physique, not only founded the presidency, but left his headship in the same manner as had the old Roman consuls — with willingness, dignity and a sense of duty done. He returned (as had Cincinnatus) to the life of a farmer. His old adversary King George III declared that this voluntary withdrawal from power was the greatest of Washington's achievements. History after all can be considered the power struggle on which may be imposed the personality traits, which may include rectitude and notable bravery or traits quite the opposite from these.

Oddly, posterity has reversed the characters and circumstances of the two presidents, making out Lincoln to be the farmer that Washington was in reality and Washington to be the politician that Lincoln really was. Washington was an outdoorsman, a man of the soil, a dedicated farmer, wilderness surveyor, and a true pioneer, a manly hero who fought in life-or-death combat. He was a soldier for 15 years, lucky to have survived it. Fleeing Indians, he jumped into an ice-covered river, swam to the other side, ran for his life through the winter woods in wet clothes. His clothes were bullet-riddled in war, sweat-drenched and rain-soaked as he managed his farm in peacetime. He is now pictured in formal clothes, powdered, be-wigged, at a formal gathering.

Lincoln is drawn as a farmer and woodsman, a pioneer, a man of the people. His present image is that of the child of low-class parents who were of no help to him. He was raised in poverty (the legend continues); was of humble Christian character; escaped his station by much self-sacrifice. That is the image embroidered by his own Republican Party and enforced after the war through relentless propaganda, despite sharply contrasting testimony from contemporaries. Says Reinhard Luthin: Lincoln "remains a subject erroneously romanticized in streams of printer ink and in the verbose speeches of politicians and civic leaders on each Lincoln Day."[3]

"With malice toward none" — to borrow one of Lincoln's most celebrated phrases — Americans can take up the task of understanding their 16th president not as myth would portray him but as he was in fact and deed. The present book attempts that daunting but vital task. The armor in which historical opinion — produced always by "the victors," as we know — has

---

[3] *Ibid.*, xi.

dressed up Abraham Lincoln is less impenetrable than it may look. We need to draw closer to it, in order to feel it.

The legend of Lincoln presupposes a figure who rose from the dust of rural America by hard and diligent struggle, working daily in the dirt, reading important books by firelight. The facts of Lincoln's life and career paint a different picture than that of the conventional narrative. He was no pioneer. From his earliest years, Lincoln ("the Railsplitter," as legend denominates him) disdained farming. "I have no farm, nor ever expect to have," he wrote in 1842 to Joshua F. Speed. "He disliked manual jobs and did no more than was necessary," says Luthin. He left home at a young age and never farmed again. It was as well, perhaps. Luthin quotes a farmer for whom Lincoln once worked as reporting that "Abe was awful lazy, he would laugh and crack jokes and tell stories all the time, didn't love work but dearly loved his pay."[4]

He was a town man. His life was spent in town pursuits. From childhood to death he loved public entertainment, as spectator or performer. He was a public entertainer, ready at any time to address an audience with stories, off-colour or otherwise. Indeed, while clerking at a store in New Salem, Illinois, where he lived from 1831 to 1837, his reputation was that of "a raconteur and arguer rather than [that of] a salesman and raconteur." Time may have embroidered that reputation. Says Luthin: "[M]ost of the humorous anecdotes and stories credited to him were not told while he lived."[5]

Lincoln's aptitude for public preening produced the expected result: namely, inattention to the nuts and bolts of daily business.

---

[4] *Ibid.*, p. 11.
[5] *Ibid.*, p. 117.

Once admitted to the bar, in 1837, he found reasons to be out and about during the long, dull hours that other lawyers spent closeted with clients or bent over volumes of the law. Rhetoric rather than research was evidently his calling. While his law partners attended to business, Lincoln ranged the district, politicking. He seems to have known more people in his district than possibly any other man.

The picture of Lincoln familiar to modern Americans is not the picture painted by his contemporaries. Not even the familiar picture of young Abe stretched lengthwise before a flickering fire, conning the best of Western literature, lacks torn places in the canvas and dark over-painting. Whereas his parents were intelligent, providing him a small library of substantive books, Lincoln's taste for those books had its limits. He appears to have read less for the love of knowledge than for the acquisition of skills likely to serve him in a public career. A future law partner, Stephen T. Logan, doubted that Lincoln "studied very much …. He was not much of a reader." A more famous law partner, William H. Herndon, said of him: "Mr. Lincoln seldom bought a new book and seldom read one." For fiction he had no appetite at all. As Luthin relates, "[H]e once confided that he had never read a novel through."[6]

Of the humility with which legend has clothed Abraham Lincoln there are no contemporaneous reports, though there are accounts of a fatalistic personality bent on (and successful at) the accumulation of money. Nor was he given to rhapsodies about the plight of the poor and downtrodden. A conservative Whig in his politics, Lincoln strongly supported the right to accumulate and hold private property. "I don't believe in a law to prevent a

---

[6] *Ibid.*, p. 10.

man from getting rich; it would do more harm than good," he once said — a sentiment that flatly contradicts the noisy egalitarianism of the early 21st century. "That some should be rich," he said in 1864, "shows that others may become rich .... Let not him who is houseless pull down the house of another, but let him labor diligently and build one for himself ...."[7]

His character was described by various associates as self-confident, aggressive, selfish, self-absorbed, consumed with ambition for power. One contemporary saw him as possessed of the sense that "he was the superior of all," with — so noted another contemporary — "a predestined work for him in the world," a thing "nobler than he was for the time engaged in."[8] His law partner Herndon described his ambition as a "consuming fire which smothered his feelings."[9] A 21st century scholar, Douglas L. Wilson, calls Lincoln "a profoundly gloomy man, troubled by dreams and other portents, and haunted by fears and apprehensions" — someone who "wanted to be remembered for doing something worthwhile."[10] Note the distinction this judgment reveals: The doing of "worthwhile" deeds would bring fame to the doer. Quiet deeds done in unlighted places were not for the likes of Abe Lincoln.

Leonard Swett — a friend of Lincoln's, be it noted — called the man "secretive," communicating "no more of his own thoughts and purposes than he thinks will subserve the ends he has in view

---

[7] *Ibid.*, pp. 128-129.
[8] *Ibid.*, p. 16.
[9] *Ibid.*, p. 23.
[10] Douglas L. Wilson, "Young Man Lincoln," in *The Lincoln Enigma: The Changing Faces of an American Icon*, Oxford University Press, 2001, pp. 28-29.

...."[11] William H. Seward, who would become his well-remembered Secretary of State, credited Confederate President Jefferson Davis with the candor his own leader lacked. Lincoln's White House secretaries and biographers, John George Nicolay and John Hay, said their employer personally politicked ceaselessly while in office, writing and reading at most one letter a day, whereas they themselves wrote much of his correspondence and some of his speeches. Such characterizations were drawn, not by Lincoln's enemies, but rather by some of his closest friends. Censures (or observations) of this sort, it seems worth noting, never speckled the reputations of Lincoln's military enemies, for instance, Robert E. Lee and Jefferson Davis. "Selfishness" was also an attribute more particularly applied to Lincoln than to his political rivals, whom he seems to have regarded as hardly less dangerous to him than were the Confederates. Ambition, the first expression of the sin of pride, was Lincoln's chief character trait.

A deep irony imbues the record of the war he began and concluded. The crushing of the Confederacy, the economic ruin of the Southern states, the dispersal of obstacles to Northern financial-industrial ambitions, the extinction of slavery, at a cost in blood exceeding that of any other American war — together these landmark occasions could be taken as one of history's greatest triumphs. All of them Abraham Lincoln saw realised on April 9, 1865, the day Lee surrendered the Army of Northern Virginia to General Ulysses S. Grant. Five days later Abraham Lincoln was dead of an assassin's bullet. The honours (such as

---

[11] Carl Sandburg, *Lincoln: The Prairie Years*, Vol. 2, Harcourt Brace & World, Inc., 1926, p. 396.

they were) of the strife and struggle were for others to sort out, the ruins for still others to pick through.

The legacy lingers, even so. He "did more than anyone else to destroy the voluntary union of free and sovereign states that was created by the founding fathers," says Thomas J. DiLorenzo, a 21st century critic, who describes the Lincoln blueprint as comprising "income taxation, protectionism, central banking, internal revenue bureaucracy, military conscription, huge standing army, corporate welfare, and foreign policy meddling."[12]

In my childhood and youth, I never heard a critical word said about Abraham Lincoln. What I learned was the orthodox Lincoln: a poor shy boy, painfully honest, from childhood stood out like a beacon in the darkness of his obscurity. He read by firelight, educated himself, aspired to nothing but Christian service. He lived a life of noble humility and saved his country when the duty to do so was forced upon him.

---

[12] Thomas J. DiLorenzo, *The Real Lincoln*, Three Rivers Press, 2002, pp. 304-305.

Origins

IT IS TIME TO BEGIN VIEWING the legend against the backdrop of the reality. Abraham Lincoln, 16th president of the United States, was born February 12, 1809, the third child of Thomas Lincoln and Nancy Hanks. The Lincoln family, of English Puritan extraction, had lived in Massachusetts, then moved to Virginia. The future president's grandfather and original American Lincoln, born in 1744, was a tanner and farmer in Virginia's Shenandoah Valley, Rockingham County, near the present Harrisonburg. During the American Revolution he served as a militia captain. In 1784 he left Virginia, settling on the Green River in Kentucky (then a district of Virginia) and acquiring extensive lands. He and his wife Bathsheba had five children — three boys and two girls. While clearing a field one day in May 1786, Abraham was shot dead by an Indian concealed in a nearby forest. Thomas, the youngest boy, then just eight years of age, stood still in shock. The oldest boy, Mordecai, ran for a loaded rifle, finding it just in time to kill an Indian (whether his father's murderer or a companion) who was poised to kill or kidnap Thomas: thereby indirectly assuring the future president's passage into the world.

In 1806, age 28, Thomas married Nancy Hanks, age 25, moved west and settled two miles south of Hodgenville, Kentucky. There Abraham was born — in the log cabin of legend. When he was two years old the family moved to five miles north of Hodgenville and settled on Knob Creek, on the main road from Nashville to Louisville. Thomas Lincoln, a carpenter, operated a tavern or inn to serve travelers on the high road that passed their front door. The family situation was not isolated. There were neighbours with children, and a steady company of lodgers in the inn. Tom Lincoln was considered a good story teller. Nancy was intelligent, serious minded. Thomas was called by some later historians a man of inferior status. In fact, he was stable, did not drink or curse, and had a benign disposition. He was an officer in his church, built the church himself, worked as farmer, carpenter, cabinet maker. He was a good citizen all his life.

Young Abraham spent happy days on Knob Creek, where his father had leased 30 acres of rich farmland. In 1816 there was a "land rush" to Indiana. Thomas Lincoln's family and Nancy's cousins, the Sparrowses and the Hankses, moved 60 miles to Indiana. They settled on Pigeon Creek, near Gentryville. Abraham did not attend school long, but his mother was serious, responsible, intelligent. The family had a good library, small in quantity, large in quality. They had many of the same books — Shakespeare, the Bible, Aesop's Fables, and so on — that were read by the future leaders of the country. They had a good dictionary, well-known biographies, standard histories, even a book of etymologies.

In 1818, when Abe was less than 10 years old, his mother Nancy died of "the milk sickness," a poison in the milk and flesh of cows that had eaten "milk weed." That disease was common then, but gradually disappeared as cultivation displaced wild plants. Nancy was 36 years old. A year later Thomas married Sarah Bush Johnston. By the accounting of everybody, including her son, Sarah was, like Nancy, much respected. Abe had another good mother, though in time to come he would rarely mention either of the two women who raised him.

Lincoln grew up to be a self-confident, aggressive character: a social leader, adept at bringing others to follow his will. And highly ambitious. He did not like the farm, field, or forest. He had a gift likewise for goading others, especially if they angered him. He had violent encounters every few years. He was a good manipulator of people and always had a cadre of followers. He was not popular with everybody but led those who allowed him.

Abraham worked for a while on the ferry at the confluence of the Anderson and Ohio Rivers. In 1826 his sister Sarah married Aaron Grigsby. A year later, she and her new-born baby died. She was 21 when she was buried in January 1828, in the graveyard at the church Thomas Lincoln had built.

Abraham was big and strong and tough — six-feet-four and lean. If strong enough physically, he was more given to reading than to the physical work that was the daily round of his contemporaries. A neighbour woman said, "He could work when he wanted to, but he was no hand to pitch in like killing snakes." John Romine said, "Abe Lincoln worked for me, but was always reading and thinking. I used to get mad at him for it. I say he was awful lazy. He would laugh and talk — crack jokes and tell stories all the time. He didn't love work half as much as his pay. He said to me one day that his father taught him to work, but he never taught him to love it."[13] He liked to sit around the store in Gentryville, where he sparkled in cracker-barrel conversation. He was considered bookish for that rustic society, but later on, among the new, literate, lawyers of the region, was labeled as a man who did not read much, knew nothing well, and was interested in books only to find a point to illustrate an argument or discourse.

He might not like to work, but he did like to fight. His dislike of the Grigsby family began when his sister married Aaron Grigsby and deepened when Sarah died, in childbirth — due, he thought, to the family's neglect. Abe kept goading the Grigsbys, ridiculing

---

[13] Douglas L. Wilson and Rodney O. Davis, *Herndon's Informants*, University of Illinois Press, 1998, p. 118.

them in humorous stories which he wrote and passed around the community.[14] The feud boiled over and erupted into a fight which Abe precipitated — his group against theirs. Lincoln, the tallest of them all, "waved a bottle of whiskey over his head, and said, 'I am the big buck of this lick' and invited a fight." A general battle followed. Lincoln challenged the smaller William Grigsby to fight him. Grigsby answered, "I know you can whip me, but if you give me fair chance I will fight you." Lincoln then asked how, and Grigsby said, "You are bigger, but I'll fight you a duel." Lincoln answered that he was not going to fool his life away with one shot. That ended the matter. That kind of event was repeated enough in Lincoln's life to have meaning. An aggressive man, pugnacious, bigger than everybody else, he was wont to seek a fist fight, to bully men shorter than himself. He took a drink when he felt like it but never learned to like it. Anecdotes abound — duly recorded by his law partner Herndon — concerning what Lincoln's friends might call his rough and ready nature, others his belligerence and touchiness. A man named Green Taylor punished him for romantic interference — Abe had apparently kissed Taylor's girlfriend — by hitting him with an ear of corn. Angry with a neighbour who had a congenital lesion on his nose, Abe dubbed the man "Blue Nose," a nickname that stayed with him for life. Once, angered by his father's dog, who barked whenever Abe tried to evade his chores and sneak away from farm work, young Lincoln sewed a coon skin to his hide, and the bigger dogs tore him to pieces. In an age when the average man

---

[14] For the encounter with the Grigsbys, see: David Herbert Donald, *Lincoln*, Simon and Schuster, 1995, p. 35; William H. Herndon and Jesse M. Weik, *Herndon's Life of Lincoln*, Albert and Charles Boni, 1930, pp. 41, 44-47.

was five feet seven inches, Lincoln was a giant, at six feet four inches. Aggressive, he was also confident. Asked about his plans for his future he answered, "I'm going to be President of the United States." Quiet sometimes he was, but not shy, not modest, never socially backward; on the contrary, socially prominent.

It was words, the tools of communication, that interested him. Any disinclination he brought to the pastime of reading vanished when his mind connected the text with the ideal of Improvement. His stepmother had brought to the family the Bible, *Robinson Crusoe*, *Pilgrim's Progress*, *The Arabian Nights*, and *Aesop's Fables*. The Hankses had preserved Mordecai Lincoln's copy of Nathan Bailey's *Universal Etymological English Dictionary*. Like William Pitt, the great British prime minister, the Lincolns admired the book and read it. Abraham read also Grimshaw's *History of the United States*, written from the New England viewpoint regarding slavery and ending with the words of the Declaration of Independence — a thrust used by Lincoln long afterwards in his speeches.

Lincoln, in Indiana, also read — slowly and repeatedly — the *Revised Laws of Indiana*. The book contained the Declaration of Independence; the Constitution, plus its first 12 amendments; the Virginia Deed of Cession, relinquishing title to the Northwest Territory; and the Northwest Ordinance of 1787, which organised government in the territory north of the Ohio River. Before Lincoln reached the age of 21, the *Revised Laws* had grounded him not only in law, but also in his personal obsession — politics.

The budding stump speaker likewise read William Scott's *Lessons in Elocution, or a Selection of Pieces, Prose and Verse*, for the *Improvement of Youth in Reading and Speaking*. The author sets forth his purpose as showing how "to convey a precise idea through such arts as simple gestures and distinctness of enunciation. The book presents famous speeches from fact and fiction, and a summary of famous maxims and selections from the classics used in public address. A similar book, *Kentucky Precepts,*" inspired him to feats of memorisation.[15]

Lincoln's step-mother said that Thomas Lincoln never made Abe interrupt reading to do any work if he could avoid it; he would do the work himself before disturbing Abe, whom he encouraged in all ways he could.

So it is clear that Lincoln combined a natural talent with a good education in his chosen field as a public man. There is strong indication that he decided to become a lawyer while still in his teenage years, while living in Indiana. He never missed a chance to practice speaking to any group, whatever the occasion.

He claimed to have spent only 12 months in school, but the record indicates a longer period. His claim totally excludes his periods of intense study, such as personally supervised tutelage by the New Salem schoolmaster William Mentor Graham when Lincoln was 24. Such books as fell into his hands were enough to educate any man: not only Bailey, Grimshaw, and Scott, but also the Bible, with its matchless instruction in style, morals, and wisdom. There were lives of Benjamin Franklin and George Washington, unsurpassed human models. There was also Sir William Blackstone's "Commentaries on the Laws of England" — a text Lincoln urged would-be lawyers to obtain and devour.

No one reading such works as these can be called uneducated. With these books Lincoln had the tools to learn style. If his literary skill derived from the training of these great works, then he is exemplary of the maxim, "It is better to read a few great books

---

[15] Lincoln's reading repertory is attested to in Wilson and Davis, pp. 806-808.

than many bad ones." He became skilled in the use of words, proving that either genetic factors or study of great literature is more important than formal instruction. His brain liked words. He liked talk, storytelling, and public speaking. He would mount a stump and preach to his acquaintances a sermon heard in church. He was a public man.

The Baptist church his family attended with such loyalty was only a mile away, but it did not attract him. He was not interested in church or religion, preferring the Bible more as a rhetorical tool than a spiritual instrument. He never joined a church or showed interest in doing so, although he made good use of Biblical quotations in his speeches. Dennis Hanks said he thought that Lincoln never believed the Bible. Other associates said that he used the Bible but did not care much for it.

He was always gregarious, pleasant, and politick, but members of his own family and close circle raised the question of how genuine or sincere he was and whether he did not have in him something of the hypocrite.

In April 1828 James Gentry sent his son Allen and Lincoln with a load of goods down the Mississippi River. They rode a flatboat on the Sangamon River to the Illinois River, thence down the Mississippi to New Orleans. Below Baton Rouge they were attacked by several Negroes, whom they repelled after a fierce fight. In New Orleans they had a good time, riding a steamboat back up the river, finally, after three months, returning to Little Pigeon Creek.

Lincoln's haunts were the public places — stores, taverns, several local courthouses — where he spent long hours talking. He read the law books, and said he wanted to be a lawyer. Law interested him mildly; politics fascinated and absorbed him.

In the area of Indiana where Thomas Lincoln lived, most people were "National Republicans," supporters of the great Henry Clay, sometime Secretary of State, senator from Kentucky, and unsuccessful presidential candidate. The Lincolns were Democrats, followers of Clay's political adversary, Andrew Jackson. Young Abraham was an enthusiastic Jackson Democrat. William Jones, the storekeeper in Gentryville, and a staunch National Republican, subscribed to the *Louisville Journal*, a Henry Clay or National Republican publication which printed selections from the New England and Philadelphia papers. These papers took the North's side against the South's on questions of tariff protection versus free trade and consolidated federal government power versus state rights. Like Clay and the National Republicans, they favoured "internal improvements" — government spending on public projects such as roads, canals, and harbors. The *Louisville Journal* denounced Jackson, who opposed the use of federal power to favour one segment of voters (e.g., capitalists) at the expense of other segments (e.g., farmers). Lincoln read the papers avidly. Political matters fascinated him. He was a political animal.

In 1828 the National Republicans backed President John Quincy Adams for re-election. His "Democratic Republican" opponent was Andrew Jackson, who in the election of 1824 had won a plurality of electoral votes, only to lose when the House of Representatives decided the contest in Adams's favour. The issues, in these years before the blossoming of slavery as the national obsession, were internal improvements and the protective tariff, a combination that Clay called the "American System." A campaign of unprecedented abuse and vilification by supporters of the two candidates concluded in a victory by Jackson.

It was during that campaign that Lincoln became a National Republican — or Whig, as party supporters renamed themselves in 1834.[16] His family attributed this change to the influence of William Jones, a Whig for whom Lincoln had clerked in Gentryville, and to the mesmerizing power of Henry Clay's speeches. Henry Clay was his idol.

Lincoln said little at this time about changing parties. Twenty-four years later, when he left the Whig Party, he was again quiet. His convictions and purposes might change. He rarely if ever advertised the changes, leaving even friends to discern for themselves the direction in which the ground had shifted. Publicly he was heard to support Jackson, but privately he was moving toward a course that would make his career and un-make the Union. Perhaps he was being his usual calculating self, concluding there was no need to create friction among his Indiana acquaintances. What is a fact is that when he arrived in his new home, Illinois, he was a Henry Clay Whig. For the rest of his life his pole star was Party, not principle. No more zealous Party man can ever have existed.

Significantly, Lincoln's own family members — who presumably knew him best — held aloof from his politics. It is reported that none voted for him in 1860 or ever joined the Federal army. The same is true of the Hanks family, save only for his second cousin John Hanks, who became a Republican when

---

[16] The Whigs took their name from the English party, dominated by members of the rising middle class, that sought to restrain the power of the king – transliterated in America as "King Andrew I of the House of Jackson." Philosophically, the Whigs were diverse: merchants and manufacturers, the wealthier Southern planters, states-rights advocates, and Western farmers desirous of internal improvements.

Lincoln was nominated and later joined the Northern army. Lincoln's own Whigs rejected him after one Congressional term in 1848. In 1860 he failed to carry his own county. It might be said that those who knew him best kept the widest distance from him, politically speaking.

NEW SALEM

THOMAS LINCOLN WAS PROSPERING in Indiana, building a new house on his farm, and busy carpentering and making furniture for the community around Pigeon Creek and Gentryville. But Nancy Hanks's cousin, John Hanks, had gone to Illinois and kept urging the family to join him. Mrs. Lincoln and other family members wanted to go, so in 1830 Thomas sold his farm and joined the migration. The Lincoln, Hanks, and Hall cousins moved together and settled together 200 miles away, in Macon County, in central Illinois eight miles southwest of Decatur, 35 miles northwest of Springfield. Abraham was 21 years old. They cleared ten acres, fenced it, built a cabin, and planted a crop. In the fall they got the "ague" — probably malaria — and then suffered one of Illinois's coldest winters, that of 1830-31.

In the spring of 1831, Abraham, John Hanks, and two other men were hired by Denton Offutt to take a flatboat of goods down the Mississippi. The trip, like the first one, was pleasant. This time there was no attack by Negroes. A myth, discredited many times, says that Lincoln saw slavery and determined that if he ever got a chance he would "hit slavery and hit it hard." Two decades were to pass before Lincoln showed much if any concern about slavery, and then only because it came into his domain of politics. "Never the apostle of a cause, he was to become the perfect interpreter of public thought and feeling and so the instrument of events."[17]

---

[17] Albert J. Beveridge, *Abraham Lincoln: A Life, 1809-1858*, Vol. 1,

Lincoln enjoyed his second three-month trip to New Orleans, returning by steamboat to work in Offutt's store in New Salem on the Sangamon River, twenty miles northwest of Springfield. New Salem was a river town, and a market and social center, possessing some stores, a tavern (inn), two doctors, several bars, and a justice of the peace, who held court. Lincoln took interest in the courts, declaring his intention to become a lawyer. At that time New Salem was in Sangamon County, later Menard County.

As always, Abraham quickly sought out and joined the local organized social groups, and quickly began to take charge. In New Salem it was the "Clary's Grove boys," a group of young men, high-spirited and boisterous. According to Dr. Jason Duncan, a physician in New Salem, "he so managed as to take complete control of them." He became their leader, using them for years as a ready and loud political claque.[18] He knew how to ask other people to attend him and his desires. Most members of a group are not themselves ambitious for power; the man who enlists their service first often acquires power easily and pre-empts a later supplicant. Lincoln was able consistently throughout his career to bring about such a result. He never stood back. It is difficult to find an individual or group association of his that he did not use to his advantage, taking more than he gave.

He liked to fight, and he liked any social activity. He drank little — less than he had in Indiana. He said the bottle robbed him of self-control. Ambition's first element is control. He had an excellent, convivial personality. He was good company, welcome at any gathering, full of stories of any coloration. His first year in

---

pp. 107-109.

[18] Wilson and Davis, p. 80.

New Salem he joined a literary and debating society, a popular outlet in those days for energy and social aspiration. One of his first acts in New Salem was to vote. Politics fascinated him. He frequented the courthouses, read law books, talked politics in the local gathering places and in the store where he worked.

Not that he enjoyed working. As we have seen, he was often called lazy. He preferred political conversation to daily business. His was a personality that naturally goes into politics, which he understood as an avenue to recognition and self-advancement, both desirable and easy of approach. Dr. Samuel Johnson was far from alone in recognising that men choose politics chiefly as a means "of rising in the world."

James Rutledge, from South Carolina, ran the tavern on the Springfield road. He was an educated man who had literary interests, owned some books, and sired ten children. He founded a debating and literary society. Abraham boarded with him and enjoyed talking to his 19-year-old blue-eyed, auburn-haired daughter, Ann — the love of his life, according to legend.[19]

Lincoln aspired to the status of Mr. Rutledge, the local doctor John Allen, and the school master Mentor Graham. He made a speech the first time he attended his debating society. He undertook to educate himself and "practiced polemics," studied

---

[19] The legend of Lincoln's supposedly lost love, Ann Rutledge – a legend that Albert J. Beveridge pronounced an "absurd myth" – would seem to be, like many myths, absurd and otherwise, quite imperishable. If nothing else it provides romantic color – with tragic overtones – to a life defined, in the public perception, by speeches and the roar of cannon. In movies and on television, Ann has been portrayed by actresses such as Una Merkel, Pauline Moore, Grace Kelly, and Joanne Woodward.

mathematics and "Kirkham's Grammar." He discussed poetry with a blacksmith who knew Burns and Shakespeare by heart.

In the spring of 1831 Thomas Lincoln bought some richer land, at Goose Nest Prairie in the southern part of Coles County, about a hundred miles southeast of Decatur. He settled on his farm and stayed there until his death in 1851. Abraham remained in Sangamon, living upon the hospitality of the Greenes, Armstrongs, and Grahams.

It was politics that intrigued him and became the focus of his studies.

In 1831 national politics was in flux. Party lines were vague. The old Federalist party of the Adamses, John and John Quincy, had died out, defeated and rooted out by the powerful Republican Party of Thomas Jefferson, which now was the only national political party. In 1824 the Republican Party had split in the bitter fight among John Quincy Adams, Henry Clay, William H. Crawford, and Andrew Jackson as candidates for the presidency.[20] "Harry of the West," as Clay's admirers had dubbed him, had won the fewest electoral votes. The House of Representatives, consistent with the Twelfth Amendment to the Constitution, was to choose among the three candidates. Clay threw his support to Adams, hoping that someday Adams's faction might return the favour, permitting him eventually to defeat Jackson. In 1828, however, Jackson could not be stopped.

---

[20] William Crawford of Georgia, backed by the most committed states' rights faction of the Republican Party, ceased to campaign for the presidency when struck down by a paralyzing illness. Notwithstanding, he received 41 electoral votes, the third largest total.

He won a big victory. Jackson's supporters began to call themselves Democrats.

Voters that year grouped around Jackson; Clay, who had become Adams's Secretary of State, to the outrage of the Jacksonians, and John C. Calhoun of South Carolina, who had won the vice presidency in 1824, running, as it was then possible to do, on both the Adams and Jackson tickets. Jackson ran as a poor common man. He was neither. Rather, he was a wealthy slaveholder who lived on a fine farm in a fine house. He was a domineering president. His personality and popularity gave him the opportunity to rule and rule he did. He opposed the Bank of the United States, which he regarded as the tool of the Eastern money interests, the industrial-financial community.

Clay, a Kentuckian, eschewed principles, devoting his career to shaping concrete policies. He later worked to reconcile differences between North and South concerning slavery. Clay, in the 1820s, called his nationalist program the "American System." It represented the banking and industrial interests in the Northeast with their support of a protective tariff to stimulate industry, a national bank to facilitate credit and exchange (or, as critics said, to allow manipulation of currency and cheap money), and "internal improvements" at federal expense to upgrade transportation between farms and cities. His program also appealed to the Western settlers, who wanted money to subsidize their new economy. He tried to solve the rising controversy over slavery by helping found the American Colonization Society to gradually free the black slaves and return them to Africa.

Lincoln, a Clay man, backed high tariffs and federal money for local public works. This transfer of money, taxing the citizen of one area, or class, to enrich another, was and still is a useful but strongly divisive action. The business community, the financial/industrial classes in the East, and the settlers in the West liked it. The farmer in the South, paying most of the federal taxes through tariffs, understandably did not like it. The people whose roots went back to the early days of the colonies opposed the Clay program on accoun1t of philosophy and experience during the Revolutionary period and thereafter. They knew that policies such as Clay advocated had produced a transfer of power from the people to the central government; enrichment of the banking and moneyed interests, which became one with the government; inflation and weakening of the currency; emptying of the Treasury; and instability and conflicts in the body politic.

The Southern colonies had opposed central government control of the economy. As states they continued the same policy. The citizen with roots in those times knew the dire result of "internal improvements." Hardly a family in the Southern colonies had escaped the ravages of debt and hardship caused by British "mercantilism" — the system whereby government sought to encourage a favourable balance of trade. The very issues which caused disaffection of the colonies from Britain were now returning to alienate South from North. The banking interests, formerly in London, were now centered in Boston, New York, and Philadelphia. Mercantilism had crossed from Old England over to New England.

The Southern colonies had opposed mercantilism, the control of trade by England, the passage of laws favouring British merchants and punishing American farmers. But in colonial days the North was hurting worse than the South. The South rushed to aid and succor to beleaguered and starving Boston, and the Revolution was begun. The relief sent by the Southern colonies to Boston in 1775 was repaid by New England, in 1861, in the coin of shot and shell. The children and grandchildren of those who benefited from Southern support in 1775 led the anti-South movement in 1861.

British tariffs had by this time become Northern tariffs. The Southern states opposed these measures on grounds of principle, injurious economic effects, and violation of clear constitutional prohibitions. They also opposed high tariffs on policy grounds, pointing to the manifest unfairness of ruling politicians' taxing one group to win the votes of another. Internal improvements for one class were paid for by another class of taxpayers. The Southern, and Democratic, position was that the central (federal) government should be a frugal government of limited powers, deriving its taxes from external trade duties. Internal taxes, the South believed, should belong to the states.

The burden of these levies was on the South. Since the days of the Jamestown colony the South had dispatched its products from plantation wharves down a hundred rivers to Europe in exchange for good cheap manufactures. Under mercantilism the British restricted trade to England so as to support their own commerce. In 1828, with John Quincy Adams as president, the North had levied a tariff (the "tariff of abominations," Southerners called it), forcing the South to subsidize Northern interests. Agriculture is a capital-hungry venture, the farmer has to wait a year for his money. The North, trying to foster commerce and industry, demanded import tariffs to raise the price of foreign goods. The tariff was both a source of revenue that did not burden the North, and also an impediment to foreign competition — in short, a preventive to free trade exactly like British mercantilism

Polarization between North and South was based on economic differences. And on a matter that stemmed directly from those differences, namely, the growing control of the central (federal) government by Northern political and economic interests.

Enter at this point Abraham Lincoln — a self-declared Henry Clay man. Henry Clay was a slaveowner, a severe critic of abolitionists as threats to the Union and had sons who were to serve the Confederacy. He was a promoter of the colonization of Negroes outside the U.S., an idea which Lincoln was to support to the end of his life.

A Henry Clay Man

LINCOLN'S CHARACTER propelled him into politics; his personality made him good at it. In character he was ambitious but lazy; he loved power even better than he loved money. He was stimulated by an audience and bored by routine. With words he was articulate, by tongue as well as pen: he would become skilled at imagery, notwithstanding frequent weaknesses in content. He could be deficient at analysis — a propagandist rather than a strict factualist; metaphorical and abstract rather than specific and practical. He could embroider and colour a vast canvas, with little interest in the accuracy of detail. Personally, he was affable, convivial, entertaining; at the same time, he lacked candor and was given to withholding his true thoughts. He spoke always for public consumption. He was a political personality, made for a political career.

In the spring of 1832, Denton Offutt's store in New Salem — where Lincoln had worked since the previous fall — failed. It was an election year. Now involved in no other business, Lincoln was free to do what he wanted to do. At age 23, he took his first step into politics, announcing not for a lesser local office, such as constable or court clerk, but rather for a seat in the state legislature.

With the usual prolonged attention that he gave his writings, he wrote his political platform in a polished style, revising and shaping until he had not only said what he wanted to say — without being dangerously specific — but said it attractively. On March 15, 1832, his announcement appeared in the *Sangamon Journal* in Springfield, 20 miles away. He would support "internal improvements," river transportation (New Salem had dreams of becoming a port city), and a legal limit on interest rates, with a way to evade the limit when necessary. He spoke approvingly of education. He ended with his customary humble and modest affect, soliciting support with the statement that if not elected, "I have been too familiar with disappointment to be very much chagrined." So, at the age of 23 years and seven months, and identified with the community of New Salem, he became a candidate for public office, a role he would perform for the rest of his life. His biographer Albert J. Beveridge wrote of him: "[T]he vagueness and dexterity of his first public utterance is the characteristic of the natural politician. He was to become the supreme exemplar. We observe, too, that cleverness and caution which distinguished his every public maneuver, and disrupted the most skillful antagonist."[21]

Throughout his life, external events uncontrolled by him acted to favour him. Lincoln was able to join with a timely public demonstration of boat transportation, riding a boat to New Salem with all the neighbourhood watching, thus being seen as the protagonist of the coming river transportation and its promise of wealth to New Salem. That nothing came of the idea is unimportant. The idea served his purpose.

A more important coincidence was the Black Hawk War, which erupted in April 1832, providing Lincoln with employment and a war record to support his run for the legislature. It was not much of a war. Chief Black Hawk and two thousand hungry Sac and Fox followers, mainly women and children, had disrupted federal

---

[21] Beveridge, p. 118.

plans to move them westward, away from lands desired by white settlers. The Indians had re-crossed the Mississippi to grow corn and feed themselves. Army troops and militiamen retaliated, driving the tribesmen into Wisconsin.

Lincoln was elected captain of the New Salem volunteer company — an event he would call, with some likely hyperbole, "a success which gave me more pleasure than any I have had since."[22] Though the unit marched into northern Illinois, it never saw combat. Captain Lincoln, no great shakes as a military man, was once placed under arrest for firing off a pistol in camp, and again court-martialed for the disorderly conduct of his men. He was required to wear a wooden sword for two days as punishment. In an odd constitutional footnote to the Black Hawk experience, Lincoln protested to his commanding officer, an army regular, that Illinois troops were at the service of the state, not the national government. His sentiments, by 1861, would swing in the opposite direction as he sought to stanch the Southern states' withdrawal from the national compact.

No more glory did he win in the election than he had in the war, finishing eighth out of 13 candidates. The brief time he spent on the stump gave him a taste he never lost for the exhilaration of the vote-seeking game. He clearly liked making speeches. He is supposed to have told voters, "My politics are short and sweet, like the old woman's dance. I am in favour of national bank. I am in favour of the internal improvements system and a high protective tariff." That placed him where he remained always, on the large-government side of the political spectrum. This was the Henry Clay position, opposed to that of Andrew Jackson.

---

[22] Donald, p. 44.

He loved campaigning, it was but an extension of his accustomed activity — talking to groups, socializing, not working. He was confident, at ease, stimulated by the opportunity. He was attractive on the stump, polling a high vote, but not quite enough to win. (Of the 13 candidates in the race, the top four won election.) Now he was burning with political ambition.

He returned to the store business in New Salem, this time with William Berry, who had been a corporal in his militia company. Lincoln gave J.R. Herndon, the previous partner, a promissory note. Everything quickly went wrong. The debt came due; the store failed; Lincoln's horse, bridle, surveying instruments, and personal effects were seized by the sheriff. When Berry died soon afterwards, Lincoln assumed his share of the debt. He appears to have paid it off in far less time than the 17 years which legend assigns to the process. The overlapping jobs he held, including that of postmaster, were no doubt a goad to his work ethic. Significantly, perhaps, Lincoln was always partial to an expansion of the money supply and the amplification of easy credit and debt.

The store at least gave Lincoln opportunity to avoid physical work, which he hated, and to talk, and to read. He had ample leisure to indulge his interests. In 1832 the newspapers that came to the New Salem post office in the store presented detailed accounts of the struggle between the national government he was later to lead and the state governments he would subdue. Years earlier George Mason and Patrick Henry had warned Virginia not to ratify the United States Constitution, with Mason arguing that the document failed to protect the interest of minorities, the Southern states in particular. "Is it to be expected," he asked, "that [the Southern states] will deliver themselves bound hand &

foot to the Eastern states?"[23] Lincoln read the state of South Carolina's historic Ordinance of Nullification, adopted November 24, 1832, declaring that in South Carolina the federal Tariff Acts of 1828 and 1832 "are unauthorised by the Constitution of the United States, and violate the true meaning and intent thereof, and are null, void, and no law, nor binding upon this State ...." The state declared that the people of a state are sovereign, warning that if the federal government applied force, South Carolina would withdraw from the Union.

On December 10, 1832, a U.S. president, as jealous of his prerogatives as Lincoln would be, declared in his own Proclamation that "The duty of the Executive is a plain one; the laws will be executed and the Union preserved by all the constitutional and legal means he is invested with."[24] Andrew Jackson could be violent when opposed. This document, written by the more facile and temperate Edward Livingston of Louisiana, acting as Jackson's Secretary of State, was a classical argument for the Supremacy of the Federal Government against secession. It was stated in a moderate and diplomatic tone. Lincoln was to use it as his model in 1861. He had leisure to learn it and to observe the superiority of a calm and quiet demeanor in such excited cases. When the occasion arose, he referred again and again to the paper of Livingston, in order to justify his powers as president.

---

[23] Jeff Broadwater, *George Mason: Forgotten Founder*, University of North Carolina Press, 2006, p. 195.
[24] Chauncey S. Boucher, *The Nullification Controversy in South Carolina*, University of Chicago Press, 1916, p. 232.

John Todd Stuart had encouraged Lincoln to try law, commending to him especially *Blackstone's Commentaries on the Laws of England*. Digging into a barrel he had bought for fifty cents, Lincoln found a copy and began studying it undisturbed. The store languished, neither Lincoln nor Berry working very hard at it. They often locked the door and left early. Whiskey was their best article of trade, selling itself. Lincoln took up surveying, which he did not like, and odd jobs. Finally, he locked the store for good. He was sued twice for debt. He followed a leisurely routine, did odd jobs, showed no interest in settled or regular work, lived with friends, usually the Greenes or Armstrongs, and travelled about the county meeting everybody.

External events came to his rescue, as they did all his life. He applied for and won a political appointment. President Jackson, although of the opposite party, appointed him postmaster at New Salem. Additionally, he was named deputy county surveyor. Contrary to myth, he was not a scholar, and he certainly did not show ability in math and science. He was fortunate to have for a teacher Mentor Graham, who in 1833 instructed him in surveying, grammar, composition, and literature, telling him, in addition, that a thorough knowledge of grammar was necessary if one wished to advance politically or socially. Lincoln had the ambition, the time, and the teachers, and by age twenty-four had achieved the motivation a younger student would have lacked.

Both jobs gave him free time to politic. He was pleased. He read all the newspapers that came to the store post office. He read more than at any period of his life. He read the anti-religious writers Comte de Volney and Tom Paine — more than he read religious works. His closest friend at the time, Joshua Speed, said Lincoln was skeptical of the Christian religion. Significantly, he never affiliated with any Christian denomination. Though Lincoln would often be called an agnostic or an infidel, Reinhard

Luthin softens the indictment, making of him "a Christian in the broadest acceptance of that term."[25]

As surveyor Lincoln met everybody in the county. His surveyor boss also told him that law, not surveying, was his talent.

During Lincoln's residence in New Salem, he held three public offices: postmaster, deputy surveyor, and member of the General Assembly of Illinois. He received good pay yet saved nothing and was negligent in the payment of debts. Lincoln was throughout his life a man who enjoyed the kindness and care of his fellow man. He was given free board and room with various acquaintances. His life was calm and slow, serene and quiet, fortuitous and fortunate during the years 1831-34. He read for utility; he practiced oratory, studied grammar and the use of words. What creates talent in certain areas is a matter not yet known to medical science but is thought to be a combination of in-born cerebral functions on which is superimposed sheer and persistent practice. Lincoln benefited both from natural talent and earnest, consistent practice. He naturally liked words. He practiced their use as play and as work. His superiority was not in moral qualities. He was no saint, no hero. His superiority lay in two qualities not of moral character but of personality: self-confidence and facility with words. Men with such qualities go far if they have the desire.

Never a worker, Lincoln was fundamentally a performer, a traveling minstrel. He told stories, wrote doggerel, composed pieces for weddings and any other event that called for public address. He was a polished teller of tales, and in every circle was the resident raconteur. Better than work he liked writing and reading, recitation, storytelling, pleasant conversation. He was a

---

[25] Luthin, p. 120.

literary technician. The spoken and written word was his medium. Not the understanding of what the words said, but rather the use of words as a means to an end was his skill. He was a communicator. He took every opportunity to perform. Rustic societies, no less than cities, produce their actors.

As he was their postmaster, members of the community came to see him. As a surveyor he got all over the county to see the community. His circle of contacts expanded widely. The two jobs illustrated his life style — he was not going to do any work that was demanding and time consuming. He would let no job interfere with his lifestyle. And he always found people to look after him so that it never became necessary for bread-winning to impede his progress. Personal fulfillment, not service, was his aim.

First Rung on the Ladder

LINCOLN WAS BY THIS TIME practicing law, though he would not be admitted to the bar until March 1837. In 1834 he ran again for the legislature. By this time party identity had become strong. Andrew Jackson was chief of the Democrats, and Henry Clay was leader of the Whigs (so called after the English political party that stood for limiting the king's powers). Jackson's opponents often referred to him as King Andrew I. The majority of Whigs — excluding States Rights Southerners who opposed Jackson over nullification — were Northeastern merchants and manufacturers, the wealthier planters of the South, and Western farmers eager for internal improvements. Jackson's successful war on the Bank of the United States and its policies had alienated many who wanted a plentiful supply of money.

Lincoln enjoyed campaigning; it was what he did anyway. Moving about Sangamon County, he spoke to entertain, making no mention of partisan issues. It was popularity he sought, and he knew how to get it. He had broad popular support. The district was heavily Democratic, and Lincoln ran as a Democrat after obtaining approval of his fellow Whigs. In Jackson country, he never once mentioned the name of his idol, Henry Clay.

Lincoln earned his legislative seat by placing second in the election, with 1,376 votes. Also elected — as a Whig — was his friend, Major John Todd Stuart, who persisted in encouraging him to consider the law as a profession. Todd had a willing listener.

Lincoln liked the law as a way of life: one that would give him prestige, income, and political contacts.

Lincoln borrowed Stuart's law books and read them until the legislature convened. He borrowed $200 from Coleman Smoot to "buy some clothes and fix up a little," leaving New Salem in style and in debt. That he, in his straitened circumstances, would buy a $65 tailor-made suit gives the measure of the man and demonstrates Lincoln's belief in the maxim, "Clothes make the man."

Abraham Lincoln was 25-years old when he rode into Vandalia to take his seat in the Illinois legislature. Vandalia had a population of less than a thousand, much increased during the legislative session. It was the political center of the state: sophisticated, more suited to Lincoln's personality than the farm village whence he came.

Lincoln and Stuart moved in together in a tavern occupied by the Whigs. Stuart was party floor leader, having served a previous legislative term. Born in Kentucky the year before Lincoln, Stuart studied law there, then moved to Springfield, where he developed a successful practice and became a prominent Whig legislator. Now he took Lincoln, and his ambitions, very much under his wing as roommate and sponsor. The chance that had come Lincoln's way did not pass unnoticed. He made good use of John T. Stuart.

The legislature convened in December 1834. Lincoln was now getting paid for what he had been glad to do at no charge — politicking. He was, as was the case throughout his career, a strong party man. He favoured all measures for internal improvements — the spending of government money for public works to benefit special interest groups. This practice of politicians, buying favour with money coerced from someone else, is older than Pericles, and grows with each nation until the nation succumbs. It is debt, and its attendant degeneracies, that destroy all civilizations.

To politics Lincoln accorded the zealous dedication that he never gave any of his store businesses. Whereas many candidates looked upon service in the legislature as an adjunct to their regular lives and merely offered their candidacies to the people, Lincoln found politics to be life itself. He traveled the length and breadth of Sangamon County, speaking in Springfield, twenty miles from New Salem, and in Petersburg. He went early to newspapers, to politicians, to people of influence, asking their favour. By the simple expedient of asking first, he was often able to pre-empt support of rivals. He took time and pains to organise. He left not a stone unturned. He enlisted the Clary's Grove boys — as in all his campaigns, continuing to the political convention for the presidency in 1860 — to talk for him, and to organize a claque at his rallies to make noise, cheer and jeer, and intimidate the assemblage.

Lincoln's style was aggressive, polemical, intensely partisan. He established a wide polarity between the rectitude, the morality of his position on the one hand, and the error, even villainy of his opponent. He did not discuss the issues in practical detail but, rather, in general and abstract terms — a safer, as well as a simpler and more attractive approach. This manner of speaking was also more difficult for the opponent to dissect and the voter to detect. He blamed all the country's ills on the Democrats — "locos" he called them, after the "Locofoco" faction in New York. (Fearing at one party meeting that opponents would turn the gas off, members of the controlling faction had provided themselves with the new "locofoco" friction matches.)

Lincoln was capable of rancor and personal abuse, but as he became more experienced he diminished the fire and brimstone, dressed his remarks in the calm style of John C. Calhoun, and while he continued to exhort the voters to hostility toward the other party he dressed his statement in a conservative style and a quiet manner. Using familiar generalities such as "Life, liberty, and the pursuit of happiness" and "all men are created equal" — phrases his lips would form at significant moments still to come — he let metaphysics mask his party politics and hide his refusal to honestly and practically treat the issues. But at this stage he was still hot. In a handbill, one opponent accused Lincoln of unscrupulous character. Lincoln came back with a handbill calling his opponent a liar and a scoundrel. He promised to give the first handbill's author a good beating if he could get his hands on him.

Lincoln was always and ever a Party regular. The Party came first. Never did he take a position that seemed likely to harm his career. With the voters he always stayed in a position that was safe. He did change his position as times changed, and did argue both sides, as lawyers do argue in behalf of whichever side pays them. He did say one thing to the voters in northern Illinois and another to those in the southern part of the state. He was a hot abolitionist and Free Soiler in talking with the Massachusetts reformers, yet he joined the Illinois voters in declaring for keeping the Negroes out of Illinois. Whatever view he gave an audience was politic, palatable, palliative. Open he was not. He never took a position that put principle before career.

On September 9, 1836, Abraham Lincoln was granted a license to practice law in the state of Illinois.

In the fall a relationship developed between Lincoln and Mary Owens. Somehow marriage came to be considered or implied. In any case, Lincoln's fervour — if any — cooled down. Mary's family was of good standing. He began behaving discourteously toward her. Once Lincoln and Mary were on a horseback ride with other young couples. Pulling up at a river, the other young men helped their lady companions across. Lincoln rode on ahead, leaving Mary to help herself across. He became moody and had nothing to say to her. [26]

In his legislative campaign he said he stood for "internal improvements." He was opposed to universal manhood suffrage but was for allowing women the right to vote. "I go for admitting all whites to the right of suffrage who pay taxes or bear arms (and by no means excluding females.)," as he put it.[27] It was a presidential election year. The Democrats nominated Martin Van Buren. The Whigs sponsored not one but three candidates, all from different sections of the country. They hoped by this tactic to thwart Van Buren's election. One candidate was the mighty Daniel Webster of Massachusetts; another, Hugh Lawson White of Tennessee. Strongest of them all, from an electoral standpoint at least, was the Indian fighter and hero of the War of 1812, William Henry Harrison of Indiana. Lincoln supported White, the Southerner.

As it happened, Illinois gave the Democrats a majority in the legislature and voted for Van Buren. But in Sangamon County the Whigs made a clean sweep, sending nine of their number — seven representatives, including Lincoln, and two senators — to the capital.

The legislature convened in December 1836 in Vandalia. Lincoln was again sick, in a state of emotional depression. He wrote Mary

---

[26] Donald, p. 68; Thomas H. Landess, *Life, Literature, and Lincoln*, Chronicles Press, 2015, pp. 205-216.

[27] Donald, p. 59.

Owens a long letter entreating her to write him, saying that he missed her and was longing for a letter. Emotional depression came to Lincoln intermittently, but nothing remitted his zeal for politics. As for Mary, she never replied.

Lincoln threw himself immediately back into the thick of Whig Party business. He quickly became associated with Ninian Edwards from Springfield, a rich and powerful Whig who had made his money in deals that were publicly questioned. Edwards was a proper Whig: imperious, eager for material gain, elitist. It was said of him that he was constitutionally an aristocrat, that he hated Democrats as the Devil hates Holy Water. Lincoln made another ally, Orville Browning from Quincy, who was possibly the only Whig to oppose "internal improvements." Twenty-five years later Browning would be appointed senator from Illinois upon the death of Stephen A. Douglas, the "Little Giant" of American politics. In the legislature Lincoln assumed the leadership of his own Sangamon delegation — nine young Whigs (including himself), aggressive, self-confident, and ambitious. Averaging over six feet and two hundred pounds, they came to be called the "Long Nine." They were active, activist, hustling for "change." With Lincoln as their leader, they persuaded the Illinois legislature to vote spending and debt for "internal improvements."

Lincoln was impressed with his own importance, and he had the ability to impress others. Under his leadership, the Long Nine led the fight for internal improvements, proclaiming that they favoured programs "commensurate with the wants of the people." Ever since politics has been practiced, ambitious politicians have instinctively known (it has not taken the reading of the lessons of history to learn it) that the quickest and surest way to rise is to stir the waters, to find an issue or a "need" of the people which, when championed, will gain notice. Next is to spend public money. That was Lincoln's method all his life, just as it was Caesar's.

Lincoln led the Long Nine in an excited campaign promoting increased government spending for an extravagant program of internal improvements. The projects were to be paid for with borrowed money and inadequate collateral — the same strategy employed by Lincoln in raising money for his three stores; namely, promises on paper. The legislature pledged the state credit for schemes of railroads, highways, river transportation, education, and other public works, all to be paid for by creating money, a practice Lincoln would follow throughout his public and private life. That Lincoln, who could not finance himself, would have the ability to understand public finance was asking much of Dame Fortune.

But it wasn't all Lincoln's fault, even though he was the leader of the movement. The years 1836-37 were a boom time, with cheap money in circulation and massive borrowing at all levels. Both Democrats and Whigs supported the policy. Amid it all, Lincoln played a prominent role as leader of the "easy money" faction in Illinois and elsewhere afterwards. He told his friend Joshua Speed that he aimed to be called the "De Witt Clinton of Illinois," after the New York governor who made a name for himself in promoting education and building railroads and the Erie Canal. The national mood was optimistic, with everybody looking to become wealthy. With cheap money came the inevitable accompaniments — speculation, specious schemes for getting rich, and irresponsible legislative attempts to overcome the laws of economics. The legislature in 1837 appropriated $10 million to subsidize a network of railroads, canals, and turnpikes intended to make Illinois prosperous. When the bill passed for these internal improvements, the people in Vandalia danced in the streets, lit bonfires, shot fireworks. Both Democrats and Whigs voted for the measure.

On the issue of the state banks, however, the Whigs and Democrats reverted to form. The Whigs were able to enact bills enlarging the powers of the state bank in Springfield and making it the state's fiscal agent. But on this issue the Andrew Jackson philosophy was affronted, and the Democrats, led by Douglas, rose up in arms. They attacked the bank as the tool of Whig elitist financiers as well as an unconstitutional monster which required slaying, not strengthening. They demanded investigation of the bank and of the process behind its establishment.

Lincoln rose to defend the bank as necessary to prosperity. He condemned its opponents. Typical of his political statements, this one did not address itself to the facts in the issue but, rather, impugned the motives of its critics. He said, "Mr. Chairman, this movement is exclusively the work of politicians; a set of men who have interests aside from the interests of the people, and who, to say the most of them, are, taken as a mass, at least one long step removed from honest men. I say this with greater freedom because, being a politician myself, none can regard it as personal."

It was indeed his personal, if widely shared, opinion. And he was, as he said, a politician. But he was pointing his finger in the wrong direction. It was the bank that was the creature of the elitist financiers. Whatever the merits of the bank in that long-ago frontier context, the mass of men have throughout history mistrusted the control of society by a small group of interlocking financial interests. And with good reason. Such schemes of selfish manipulation always come to evil.

A legislator named Linder had merely introduced a resolution to study the matter of the state bank, suggesting that the bank was so fiscally weak that it could not afford to pay the sums for which Lincoln's internal improvements program had obligated them. Lincoln attacked Linder with ridicule and withering scorn.

This episode demonstrated Lincoln's political style. Every issue was a political contest, every campaign a fight. He early adopted and never rejected a highly partisan style. He made unsubstantiated charges, branding opponents as villains, enemies of the working man, opposed to the "good." He would accuse an opponent of some act or statement that had neither occurred nor been uttered. The effect, of course, was to throw the opponent into a position of constant defense.

His quiver was full of the arrows of hyperbole, and he shot them broadside. He could not speak without attacking his opponent as evil, accusing him of some imaginary vice. He always drew his opponent and the opposing position in caricature, and often did it so attractively and repeatedly that the caricature came to be perceived as the truth. While attacking his foe he evaded any specific, unequivocal statement that would identify his own position. He straddled the issue, always leaving himself a safe retreat. He carefully avoided any public statement that would give him a clear ideological identity. He always chose abstraction and religious metaphor rather than a definite treatment of the facts. This was true of his law practice as well as his politics, described by colleagues as short on facts, long on courtroom performance.

Lincoln led another fight in the legislature, as bitter as any over "internal improvements." This concerned a resolution which he and other Whigs advanced to remove the capital from Vandalia to Springfield, Lincoln's home territory. The majority of settlers in Illinois were from the Southern states and settled in the southern part of Illinois. New immigrants were now coming in from the Northern states and settling in northern Illinois. Lincoln and the Long Nine led an effort to move the capital to the north. This fight was as bitter as the other two. The issue was pure politics. It required much "logrolling" — promises to support whatever internal improvements were sought by legislators who might vote for the move. With the use of "logrolling" money and the votes of legislators who lived closer to Springfield, the bill passed. Most of the votes came through trades and promises. Victors and vanquished alike recognized Lincoln as the chief strategist. Gen. L.D. Ewing accused Lincoln of accomplishing his aims through deals and use of taxpayer money to gain personal objectives. Lincoln returned fire in a blistering speech full of personal abuse. Gen. Ewing challenged him to a duel. Lincoln's emissaries were able gradually to assuage his anger and eventually induce him to dismiss the challenge. The bill passed. Vandalia lost.[28]

On February 28, 1837, a joint session declared Springfield to be the new capital, with the government scheduled to move there officially in 1839. That night a boisterous victory celebration was held in the tavern. The guests enjoyed free champagne, cigars, oysters, and a sumptuous dinner, financed by railroads, contractors, land speculators, and private interests that stood to profit from the move. The celebration cost an enormous (by standards of the day) $600. Legislators, being human, never change, it seems. At least 81 bottles of champagne were consumed. Lincoln was hailed as the hero in the successful

---

[28] *Ibid.*, pp. 62-63.

accomplishment of the related programs of internal improvements and capital relocation.[29]

John Todd Stuart had invited Lincoln to join his law practice in Springfield. Lincoln readily accepted. It had probably already been in his mind to move to Springfield. New Salem was losing population as its river traffic declined and economic activity shifted elsewhere. Springfield, 20 miles away, was a commercial center, soon to become the capital of a fast-growing state. Life there was an alluring prospect to a lawyer. Moreover, the town was grateful to Lincoln for his leadership in giving them the capital and would certainly reward him for it. To be part of Stuart's vigorous practice guaranteed success. Lincoln looked forward to this rise to a higher rung on the ladder.

The legislature adjourned on March 6, 1837, leaving Vandalia to wither. Lincoln went home with the Long Nine, bantering and joking all the way. A dinner was held for them when they arrived in Springfield, with Lincoln as the honoured member. Those who had benefited from his legislative work feted him. One toast ran: "Abraham Lincoln: he has fulfilled the expectations of his friends and disappointed the hopes of his enemies." Lincoln's words were on the subject of friends and enemies, "We" and "They." He was always a partisan man, and the enemy was always the other party. On the short trip from Springfield to New Salem he was again feted, in Athens on the way. Contemporaries called him a "born politician."

---

[29] *Ibid.*, p. 64.

"Emancipating Slaves"

ONE MORE AGENDUM in the legislative session of 1836-37 gave insight into Lincoln's political position. The legislature received memorials from several Southern states expressing concern about the rising activity of the small but increasingly hostile abolition groups in the North. These memorials asked the Northern states to recognize the threat to the harmony of the federal union posed by dangerous and radical doctrines sure to bring about sectional hostility. Sectional rivalry existed already due to political and economic differences. The abolitionists had formed the American Antislavery Society for the purpose of converting Northern opinion from tolerance of slavery.

Southerners were alarmed at the ultimate consequences of the work of zealots, as they saw them, whose purpose was not to solve a problem but, rather, to attack an institution and a region that were, to them, mere abstractions. They demanded that the slaves be immediately and unconditionally set free. Southerners knew the theoretical and practical objections to their peculiar institution. Yet there were competing considerations. As Southerners saw it, Northerners bore some culpability for slavery, having taken delivery of black Africans from other black Africans, then transporting to the colonies — amid degrading conditions — those who were to be sold on the auction block. Southerners noted as well that, climate and soil having conspired against the success of Northern slavery, the institution became all but extinct north of the famous Mason-Dixon Line. A slave-less North and a slaveholding South could not be counted on to compose their differences easily.

The new opinions on slavery's unsuitability were by no means general in Northern circles. For the great majority of Northerners, slavery was not yet an issue. Many seem to have feared the collapse of social order in the event of emancipation. Except for Massachusetts, where only a handful of Negroes lived, most Northern states had enacted "black laws" separating the two races in society.

Illinois was typical. A few settlers in Illinois who had come from New England favoured abolition; many more seem to have feared that abolition would bring in Negroes from the neighbouring states of Kentucky and Missouri. Illinois had its own — as they would later be called — "Jim Crow" laws, which made it difficult for a Negro to enter the state. Later on, Illinoisans voted overwhelmingly to prohibit any more Negroes from entering the state. Nor could Negroes vote in Illinois or sit on juries. Lincoln voted for that measure.

In January 1837, the Illinois legislature, with near-unanimity, adopted resolutions calling Abolitionists a dangerous and reprehensible menace to the Union, affirming the constitutional right of slave ownership, pronouncing slavery a state institution specifically outside federal power, and declaring that "the General Government cannot abolish slavery in the District of Columbia against the will of the citizens of said District." Lincoln and another Sangamon County Whig, Dan Stone, who had accounted for two of the six House votes against the resolutions, composed their own protest against slavery and had it recorded in the House Journal on March 3, 1837.

They took their stand with the radical Northern Whig faction. They agreed that the federal government had no right to interfere with slavery in the Southern states but that "the Congress of the United States has the power, under the constitution, to abolish slavery in the District of Columbia; but that power ought not to be exercised unless at the request of the people of said District." Lincoln extricated himself from trouble by criticizing the Abolitionists, but he had embraced an abstraction that became the "general idea" of his time. The legislature's anti-abolitionist resolutions were enacted in January 1837. Lincoln did not write his pro-abolition statement until March 3, three days before adjournment, when little notice could be taken of his heterodoxy.

History's hindsight in this context makes Lincoln out as more opportunist than abolitionist. He tested the wind, then trimmed his sails. He followed the crowd to become its leader. He was a politician first, unwilling to let the issue hurt him, but he had sided with those who in the course of a few decades would plunge the nation into crisis and division.

The most difficult subject in American history is that of Negro slavery. The human mind has great limitations and after attending to its own personal, selfish requirements has little time for, and less comprehension of, external events. Distant events, whether distant in space or time, are viewed simply by most men. Therefore, to anybody not personally involved with slavery the idea of slaveholding is so repugnant that it is logical to agree with the Abolitionists that it should be abolished, extirpated, cut away, and exterminated regardless of the complications of the operation. Even if the operation kills the patient.

So it came to pass in 1865. The operation killed the patient. The South fell into economic ruin Three quarters of a million Americans — in a population of 31 million — purchased the outcome with their lives. The conflict had other enduring results. The United States of America became a very different kind of nation than it had been throughout most of its comparatively brief history — with manufacture and banking as the economic driving forces; with a powerful, domineering central government replacing the looser, locally oriented confederation put into place by the founding fathers.

Once established, slavery was the monetary capital, the store of value of the entire slaveholding region. This made the fate of the institution a more delicate and complex matter than abolitionists commonly made it out to be. It was one thing to talk of instant freedom, another thing entirely to sort through the vast consequences and implications of such a doctrine. A reasonable man, a moderate, a man of good will, a man who was anything like what Lincoln is called by history, would have understood such obvious facts.

Lincoln was an abolitionist when it suited him. Lincoln was not a moderate on the slavery issue; he was a politician who knew he had better appear to be a moderate if he expected to win government office. Lincoln was a human being and capable of only the limited view controlled by self-interest — the view that directs most men.

Abolitionist activity was rising fast, fueled by Northern capitalist and political interests needing an issue to neutralize the agrarian South. John Quincy Adams, a man of Massachusetts even after his service as president of the United States, scourged the Democrats with the abolitionist whip. He was abolition's political leader, attributing every position the South (i.e., the Democratic party) took in the Congress to the "evil of slavery."

The issue of slavery burned hotter as the abolitionists, businessmen, and politicians of the North banded together in common interest. In Springfield, resolutions were adopted calling abolitionists "dangerous," "designing," and "ambitious" men. In November 1837 Elijah Lovejoy, an abolitionist editor, was shot by an Illinois mob that dumped his printing press into the Mississippi River. It bears repeating that the mob's members were residents of a free, not a slave, state.

Lincoln, for all the comparative moderation with which he spoke, reinforced the abolitionist cause at nearly every turn.

On January 27, 1838, Lincoln demonstrated the basis of his political position in a speech to the Young Men's Lyceum, in Springfield. The speech was motivated by the murder of Elijah Lovejoy, although Lincoln did not mention him by name. Like the abolitionists, Lincoln, throughout his career, preferred the Declaration of Independence, a political apologia, for all its fame and distinction, to the Constitution, his nation's governmental charter.

As was his rule he covered his message with a veil, in this case a veil of careful objections to violence. The abolitionists claimed morality and peace on their side, but they were in fact fomenting revolution against the social order in half the nation. The young legislator who, as president, would commence the nation's bloodiest war, deplored mob violence without raising the urgent question, whence the appetite for violence? Who, to put it another way, had scattered sparks on dry tinder — proslavery people by virtue of maintaining an institution neither approved nor condemned under the constitutional order? Or had antislavery people done so by demanding that others' wills be bent to their own?

The intonations of the Lyceum Address — reverent, high-minded — foreshadowed those of the Gettysburg Address 25 years later. There were no overt accusations, but in Lincoln's s telling, the authority of the Founding Fathers fell on the shoulders of those who opposed slavery: those against whom violence had been done yet who themselves had done no violence. Apart, that is, from urging the overthrow of the existing order.

In the history of nations, Lincoln said, there was a time for passion, and a time for restraint and rational debate. America had had her time for passion in the Revolution, which used "the jealousy, envy, and avarice incident to our nature" to create out of the blood and fire of war a nation based on equal rights and self-government. And now, in order to preserve and consolidate their experiment, America no longer needed that kind of passion. What the people needed was "Reason, cold, calculating, unimpassioned reason." Let them "swear by the blood of the Revolution" to respect and obey the laws and stop the violence. Let reverence for the law be sung by every mother to her child, "let it be preached from the pulpit, proclaimed in legislative halls, and enforced in courts of justice. And in short, let it become the political religion of the nation, and let the old and the young, the rich and the poor, the grave and the gay, of all sexes and tongues, and colors and conditions, sacrifice increasingly on its altars."

Fine sentiments, these. Who could disagree? What they masked was the growing attachment of abolitionists such as Lovejoy to anarchy, illegality, illiberality, and intolerance. Such characteristics could hardly solve the enormous problem to which the abolitionist cause had addressed itself. The problem, under the ministrations of the abolitionists, could only grow more acute.

Lincoln invoked the imagery of the altar and the church — institutions by which he set small store. He made good use of the idiom of his time. This was his view, and that was his method: stirring words for a speech to a lyceum, effective for a political candidate, but impractical in an honest man, and irresponsible in a statesman truly devoted (as he said he was) to peace. The South had had a remarkably tranquil social order. Its peace now was being disturbed by the abolitionists.

One passage in the Lyceum Address, viewed from the distant future, is clothed in irony.

Men of talent and ambition will spring up amongst us. And when they do they will as naturally seek the gratification of their ruling passion, as others have done before them .... It thirsts and burns for distinction. And, if possible, it will have it, whether at the expense of emancipating slaves or enslaving freemen. Is it unreasonable then to expect, that some man possessed of the loftiest genius, coupled with ambition sufficient to push it to its outmost stretch, will at some time, spring up among us? And when such a one does, it will require the people to be united with each other, attached to the government and laws, and generally intelligent, to successfully frustrate his designs. [30]

---

[30] For the Lyceum Speech, Abraham Lincoln, *Speeches and Writings*, The Library of America, Vol. 1`, pp. 28-36; Donald, pp. 80-83.

SPRINGFIELD: A BIGGER STAGE

IN APRIL 1837 LINCOLN rode into Springfield on a borrowed horse, with $7 in his pockets, owing more than $1,000. Money, debt — personal or public — rarely worried him. Aggressive man that he was, he was able to have his needs amply supplied by others throughout his life.

He was in a good mood, a hero to the 2,000 inhabitants of Springfield, and ready to collect on their gratitude for giving them the capital.

He got a bed with Joshua Speed over Speed's store, at no charge, and took his meals, also free, at the home of Bill Butler, one of the Long Nine.

Stuart and Lincoln's office was over a store where circuit court was held, on the town square. They had a successful practice. But, as happened so often to Lincoln, and to other men of ambition, his rise to a higher level of success failed to satisfy him or give him the pleasure he expected. His restless ambition looked around for higher rewards. He told friends what he had said when elected to the legislature and would say later about other honours, including election to Congress: to wit, he was surprised at his lack of satisfaction in the attainment. For Lincoln success did not satisfy; if anything, it depressed. He called his life in Springfield "dull." Socially, he was popular; politically, he rose fast. He was making money in a successful law practice before he was 30 years old. Still, he was not content.

Lincoln and John Stuart had a successful law practice, both economically and politically. Stuart was running for Congress and Lincoln for the legislature. Lincoln's political engine never rested. He was an untiring worker and a leading member of the Whig party, always in the middle of its activities. With Democrat Reuben Radford he had an argument, saying later that he had wanted to hit him, and but for the presence of Radford's friends he would have carried out his desire to "knock him down and leave him kicking." He was called vulgar and rude in argument. He cursed when he felt like it, even in public print. He was criticized repeatedly for vulgar and untrue statements.[31] He was an important part of the group, any group: the Lyceum, the Whigs, the gathering at the store, and the rowdies. Lincoln had to lead. If the group would not play the game his way, he would not play it. He and some others attacked a drunkard who had hurt his wife, tied him to the courthouse pump, and gave him a beating.

As he was center of a group, the center of his life was politics. He loved it and lived it. He was a Whig leader, made speeches, wrote any kind of tract — from pious to scurrilous — for the Whigs, The Whigs met in the office of the *Sangamon Journal*, a Whig paper operated by Simeon Francis, Lincoln's close ally and friend. Lincoln was aggressively proud of his position in the Whig inner circle.

To the Whigs the villains were the Democrats, led by Stephen A. Douglas, possibly one of the ablest, most underestimated political figures of the 19th century. Douglas's father, a doctor in Vermont, had died when Stephen was a child. The boy was apprenticed as a cabinet maker, just as Lincoln's father had been. He came west, taught school near Jacksonville, Illinois, and then became a lawyer. He was an Andrew Jackson Democrat, opposing the

---

[31] Wilson and Davis, p. 475.

National Bank and the elitist financial clique which led the Federalist-Whig group. Douglas was an achondroplastic dwarf, victim of a disease that ran in his family, characterized by short stature due to a deficiency of pituitary growth hormone. He was deficient in little else, being intelligent, vigorous, articulate, and straightforward. He had been admitted to the Illinois bar in 1834, became attorney general and legislator for Illinois, and in 1837 registrar of the Springfield Land Office. Douglas' height — at least a foot shorter than Lincoln's — afforded a perfect visual image of an opponent and the dream of caricature.

The Young Democrats, led by Douglas, and the Young Whigs, who were steered in practice by Lincoln, were social clubs with a goal. They had fun, but with a deadly aim — political power. No force can weld together a group like self-interest.

The Young Whigs were the center of Lincoln's life, and he was at the center of theirs. Lincoln was his party's writer. He produced whatever the party needed, and it was coarse and rough when he wanted it to be. A Democratic candidate for county judge accused the Whigs of conspiracy to destroy him. Lincoln wrote a vicious letter to the editor calling the Democrat "false as hell," saying he was not a lawyer but a "liar." Lincoln's attacks knew few limits. His quiet phase was yet to come, in the years 1847 and 1848, which he spent in Congress observing John C. Calhoun.

In 1838 Lincoln won re-election from Sangamon County to the legislature. His partner Stuart was elected to Congress, defeating Stephen A. Douglas. Indicating that he was not going to split his income with Stuart while Stuart was away in Washington City, Lincoln wrote in the account book, upon Stuart's departure,

"Commencement of Lincoln's Administration."[32] His idiom, his very concepts were political.

He had lost interest in Mary Owens and discharged her by the classical technique of skillfully letting her know he was not interested: at the same time, allowing her to believe that the separation was her decision. He told her that he was just not the right man for her, that he was poor and confused in his mind. He gave plenty of reasons for her to resign him, the real one being his lack of interest. His rhetoric to Mary was not unlike his calculated diversionary political expressions. When she finally did break off the relationship, he wrote his friend Mrs. Orville Browning (wife of the man who would be appointed U.S. senator when Stephen Douglas died), a cruel satire on the Mary Owens affair. Mary's unhappiness never troubled him.

Springfield was a vigorous municipality. Commercially lusty, growing, the government center, it offered a number of schools, a lecture circuit, a Thespian Society, and a Young Men's Lyceum which Lincoln joined. There were six churches, the center of social life, which Lincoln did not join. His exclusion of the church from his life was more than the common apathy of youth. He was philosophically opposed to the church — a follower of the popular general ideas of his day that came in the wake of the 18th century Enlightenment, with the large questions of sin and redemption postponed for contemplation by those who cared

---

[32] Lincoln's political skills, forged alike from native ability and constant practice, are comprehensively attested to in the Lincoln literature. Richard Current sums up Lincoln as "a politician's politician, a manager of the party machine, a wire puller – in short such a 'contriver' as he professed not to be." Richard N. Current, *The Lincoln Nobody Knows*, McGraw Hill, 1958, p. 211.

about such things. There was something of the Calvinist about him in terms of the haunting anxieties he carried about yet never worked out — possibly never tried hard to work out. "He did not believe," says Douglas C. Wilson, "in personal salvation or redemption."[33] As a man of the Enlightenment, he took naturally to the notion of Reason — whatever such a term, dripping in ambiguity, might mean — as man's most trustworthy guidepost. "Reign of Reason, all hail!" he cried in an 1842 address. Yet, paradoxically, he was given to superstition and fatalism. In the rivalry of church and state his loyalties lay with the state and never changed. That fact has been lost on historians.

In 1837 a financial "panic" — a depression, we would call it now — struck the United States. This economic phenomenon is a liquidity crisis, a shortage of money due to debt created by previous expansion of the money supply by governmental policy. Politicians, it seems, are never able to resist courting the quick popularity brought on by "easy money." For a time it looks good. Certainly the people look — and feel — happy. But eventually the money supply is exhausted. Government alone can increase the money supply. Government alone can cause inflation that precedes and produces depression. A "panic," it should hardly be necessary to point out after decades of experience, is always caused by government. Nevertheless, government too infrequently receives the blame it deserves. More often than not, instead of falling on the perpetrators, responsibility comes to rest — in the public's mind — on those whose task it becomes to clean up the mess.

In 1837 business, banks, governments, and people began to run out of money, unable to pay their debts. State governments in the

---

[33] Wilson, pp. 27, 31.

Midwest began to default on their loans and to halt their programs of internal improvements. Lincoln not only opposed reduced spending, but urged increasing debt, oblivious or uncaring as to what would happen to state bondholders, and ignorant of the fact that the state would be unable to sell new bonds (raise new money) when they were unable to pay on the old ones as interest came due. Lincoln's monetary irresponsibility was a hallmark of his political outlook.

He spent his time polishing the arts political. In the evening he gathered with a crowd in Speed's store talking politics and telling stories. Lincoln was the acknowledged leader in this act of the political drama, a consummate jester and performer, practicing what was natural to him and necessary to the politician. Whatever the colour — "off" or "on" — of his stories, he repeated them all with relish, practice improving an inborn talent.

He read mostly newspapers. Current politics was the subject. He read law, superficially according to the other lawyers, but sufficient to his needs. He did read some poetry, again with particular attention to learning how to polish his own rhetoric. He was interested in style, in being able to say his speeches attractively, word for word. That was his essential talent, the principal quality of this man — the ability acquired by nature, and improved by nurture, to write politically, to compose literature. He was not a great thinker, but he was indeed a great declaimer. He was no Christian and no moralist, but he used both avenues to his ends. As a politician he drew references to both. That was his political method — beautiful communication.

During the years 1837 through 1839, as we have already noticed, the nation suffered from a severe financial "panic," one of those acute shortages of money which inevitably follow the irresponsible government policy of increasing the money supply. The nation was in an uproar. Individual citizens, banks, businesses, and governmental bodies were going bankrupt. The state bank in Springfield suspended "specie" or hard money payments. That is, they would no longer pay in gold or silver — money with a more reliable store of value — but would redeem only with paper. The Illinois legislature met in three sessions from 1837 to 1840 to consider the problem. Lincoln, serving as Whig floor leader of the House, led a majority vote which he used to curtail current internal improvement projects while enacting additional canal and railroad projects. His argument was that such projects would provide employment and stimulate the economy. He would solve problems caused by debt, by creating more debt.[34] Lincoln was now a strong Whig boss. He ran for speaker of the House but lost to a Democrat whom, during the campaign, he had called "not worth a damn."

In the winter of 1839-40 the legislature met in Springfield for the first time. The financial crisis dominated the proceedings. The state debt was now $10 million, with annual interest of $600,000 which the state was hard-pressed to find. Lincoln fought for a continuation, even an expansion, of government works. He said he would have his legs ripped off before he would abandon that policy. The legislature voted to continue existing programs of public works but not create any new ones. They enacted a general property tax which Lincoln gladly endorsed.[35]

He used his influence in the Whig party to renew the charter of the floundering state bank, partly from policy, more urgently because many of his Whig friends were in debt to the bank and would otherwise have their loans called. Lincoln never could manage his own personal finances. It is unlikely that such a man

---

[34] Donald, p. 74.
[35] *Ibid.*, pp. 76-79.

could have mastered public finance. His policy was imprudent and impractical but always the same: Spend more, create more money. For his entire career, the effect of his conduct in finance was to weaken the currency and cause economic distress. This time he had a new scheme for raising more money to fund more internal improvements. He would have the state of Illinois buy 20 million acres of federal land, at 25 cents an acre — and then sell it off at $1.25 an acre. The legislature adopted it, but Congress did not.

In October 1839, the Whig Party met in Springfield and endorsed William Henry Harrison for president. Out of the meeting came a Whig State Central Committee, consisting of Lincoln and four close friends. They published a Whig paper, its name pointing to Harrison's 1812 War fame as the "Old Soldier." Lincoln created a secret, detailed program to organize the whole state down to each precinct, with instructions telling each county committee how to woo the voters and transport all Whig voters to the polls on election day. There were no issues, either spontaneous or politically created; the campaign, accordingly, was one of personalities.

DEPRESSION

IN THE EARLY DAYS OF ILLINOIS, a man named Ninian Edwards had settled there. He was a Kentucky judge appointed by President Madison as first governor of the territory of Illinois. When Illinois became a state, he became senator. Edwards involved himself in the web of banking, land speculation, and politics that had made so many men rich. Though accused of numerous acts of embezzlement and corruption, he was never convicted. He became governor in 1826, bought land for delinquent taxes, and lived out his life having attained his goal of money and power. His son, Ninian W. Edwards, was one of the Long Nine, a friend of Lincoln's. The two had campaigned all over the state together.

Edwards had married Elizabeth Todd, daughter of Robert Todd of Lexington, president of the Bank of Kentucky. Elizabeth's younger sister Mary Ann came to Springfield to visit the Edwardses. In December 1839, at a cotillion, she met Abraham Lincoln. Mary, then 21 years old, the fourth of seven children, was intelligent and interested in matters of the intellect, witty with a lively personality. She attracted Lincoln, who was nearly 10 years her senior; likewise, he attracted her. She liked politics, was a Whig herself, and knew well Henry Clay, a friend of her father. Henry Clay, Lincoln's model and idol!

Her mother had died when Mary was six. Her father married again and had nine more children. Mary loved her father and enjoyed his prominent life in the socially and culturally elevated Lexington. Robert Todd was a slaveowner, and the family was raised in intimacy with coloured people. Mary thought slavery an imperfect system but believed their servants were better off enslaved than turned out into the world on their own.

Three of Mary's cousins had gone to Illinois: John J. Hardin, John T. Stuart, and Stephen Logan. Lincoln would battle one of these men — Hardin — for political office. With the other two he would practice law. Mary joined the social whirl centered on Springfield and the Edwards family. Compared to Lexington, Springfield was "less orderly, but fun," as Mary put it, with the attractions of "glitter, show, and pomp and power" as a vulgar and ambitious society looked for future rewards. Stephen A. Douglas came to see her some, but no intimacy developed.

In 1840 Lincoln was re-elected to the Illinois legislature, and his partner John T. Stuart to the U.S. Congress. The year 1840 was a significant one in American politics. The Whigs won the presidency, though the victory later went sour. Harrison promised to be what his successor John Tyler proved to be, and what neither had ever denied being — conservative. The Eastern and Northern financial-industrial interests, and the ambitious men who wanted the government to spend tax money to their benefit, were disappointed in their leaders and turned against them in a period which demonstrated the polarity in United States political history that finally led to war.

"Internal improvements" was but a vague title for improper use of government money and power. The protective tariff, the U.S. Bank and state bank practices, and use of the government for private personal gain — these constitute the story of government. These realities in 1840 and afterwards marked another step toward division and war. The Northern interests detested the president's limited government policy. John Tyler — who had taken office upon Harrison's early death — spoke of himself as "an outlaw to my own party." With an enviable sense of humour, considering the circumstances, he changed the name of his home to "Sherwood Forest," identifying himself with the famous bowman and outcast.

But none of this concerned 31-year-old Abraham Lincoln. The political campaign of the Whigs, and his campaign for the hand of Mary Ann Todd, consumed his interest.

Lincoln spared nothing in political work. No prominent issues attracted the public's attention, so the 1840 campaign was focused upon the usual adversarial claims and attacks. Lincoln's Whigs called the Democrats the party of the high class and the Whigs the party of the people. They called Van Buren a fancy-dressed aristocrat who lived in luxury. They claimed Harrison was born in a log cabin and drank cider. This was not true but is an intimation of the later incarnation of Lincoln as the "Rail-Splitter."

Douglas and Lincoln now had their first public debates. In the legislature Douglas attacked the Whigs' economic policies and blamed them for the financial depression. Lincoln defended the U.S. Bank and blamed Jackson and Van Buren for national bankruptcy and corruption. Another of his aggressive and heated speeches gained him notice. This one was published for use in the campaign and in a Washington newspaper, the *National Intelligencer*, in August 1840.

Lincoln, ever the showman, in one of his speeches did an act imitating one of the Democratic candidates. He overdid it, made himself look foolish, and he apologized for it. He was learning from the greatest teacher — experience. But he still engaged in fights and intemperate polemics.

The *Sangamon Journal*, owned by Lincoln's intimate Simeon Francis, accused Douglas of devotion to the cause of Africa's sons and being pro-Negro. Douglas accused Harrison of being soft on abolition. Lincoln accused Van Buren of being an abolitionist. He quoted a Van Buren biography showing that Van Buren had once voted for Negro suffrage in New York. Mainly, Van Buren was a politician. Van Buren had voted against abolition in the District of Columbia, but later, angered by the election of the Tennessean James K. Polk to the place he sought, he led the split.

Van Buren's frustrated ambition separated Northern from Southern Democrats. This selfish act — the embrace of power in preference to principle — was one of the bases of Lincoln's election 20 years later. The voters believe that politicians are idealistic, but the fact is that most politicians give every evidence of being motivated by the power drive. Politicians are members of a club which holds regularly scheduled, giant athletic contests. The entrants know that the race is not always to the swift or the deserving, but that the rewards for the lucky winner are enormous. The prize is the greatest the world can offer — worldly power. Between contests, the athletes — the competitors — band together, compare notes, and enjoy themselves. The winner of the first prize bestows hundreds of prizes upon his party fellows, and the voters never know it.

Lincoln devoted his public time to campaigning. He went to all the Whig rallies and spoke wherever he could. His law practice was successful. He won and lost cases, but he prospered. He appeared before the Illinois Supreme Court in January 1840. But, although law was the profession that made his living, it was politics and personal life that made his living enjoyable.

He and Mary Todd were attracted to each other. She was intelligent, witty, sociable. He was political if not exactly politick, making a good living; the kind of man who will get ahead. Quickly Mary saw in him that hard vein of ambition. She was confident, as he was, that he was going to rise.

The election year of 1840 was a busy one for Lincoln. He worked tirelessly for the Whigs and was romantically busy with Mary Todd. He and she were part of a social-political group that worked and played together for the rest of their lives. Mary's best friend, Mercy Ann Levering, lived next door to Mary. Her beau and future husband was James C. Conkling, a lawyer and Princeton graduate who worked in the Whig group. They exchanged confidences. Mary called Lincoln "the most congenial man she had ever met." She liked him and his political way of life. In December they planned to be married.

The romantic life and the political life did not inhibit each other. No Whig did more for the party in 1840 than Lincoln, who had the ability and, what is more important in politics, the desire to do the work. He showed energy in organising and talent in speaking, and unceasing activity. William Henry Harrison's politics, in contrast with Lincoln's, were those of a conservative, an exponent of small government. At least he was a fellow Whig. Lincoln was a party man utterly from the beginning of his career. He remained so much a party man that at the consummation of his career — election to the presidency — he received not a single popular vote in 10 Southern states.

To Lincoln the enemy was always the other party. He travelled the state over, fighting for his party. The Democratic presidential candidate, Van Buren, whom Lincoln labeled an aristocrat, was more like Lincoln politically than Harrison was. That didn't matter to Lincoln. Van Buren made one mistake: he opposed many spending schemes in the Northwest, in an attempt to correct the financial crisis. His decision lost him Illinois, the Northwest, and the 1840 election. Lincoln would never make the mistake of throwing away an election in defense of fiscal solvency. A Democratic newspaper had sneered at Harrison for his supposed humble origins. His origins were not humble at all, but the sneer helped him. There was nothing much to say about Harrison. He was not a strongly partisan politician. He had been a soldier; he was honest. He came from a family prominent in Virginia's history.

Lincoln, a Whig elector, voted for Southern-born Harrison. So did Illinois and the nation. The economic depression, the fall in land values, and Van Buren's opposition to Western money projects were too much for Van Buren to overcome; he failed of re-election. The Whigs did get a victory, but as with their victory later with Zachary Taylor and Fillmore, it failed to satisfy the Whig political core — the monied political group which wanted strong government, high tariffs, government spending (i.e., internal improvements), and debt.

Lincoln and Mary — "Mollie" he called her — decided in December to get married. But, again, the prospect of marriage affrighted him. He became gloomy, depressed.

As if romantic turmoil were not a sufficiently consuming occupation, he found himself buffeted by political whirlwinds. The legislature opened its 1840-41 session in the Springfield Presbyterian Church. The Democrats were trying to terminate the State Bank because it had quit paying in specie. Led by Lincoln, legislators authorised the bank to continue operating. Lincoln continued his role in bringing about the financial distress brought on by internal improvements, money creation, and a debt of $14 million. Emergency measures kept the state afloat financially. Lincoln introduced a bill requiring school teachers to pass an examination and be certified to teach. The bill, representing one of his few forays into education policy, was duly enacted.

The wedding of Abraham Lincoln and Mary Ann Todd was scheduled for January 1, 1841. All was in readiness on the appointed day — all but the intended groom, who failed to show up.

A period of mental and emotional anguish had commenced. For a week after defaulting on his commitment to Mary, Lincoln stayed in bed. He was treated by Dr. Anson Henry, a physician upon whom Lincoln became dependent, for "hypochondria," a non-specific term, meaning literally a "distress below the chest," and referring to emotional depression. Dr. Henry was so attentive that Lincoln urged him not to carry out his intention to move away from Springfield. Lincoln made persistent efforts, using his political connections, to have Dr. Henry awarded the postmastership to augment his income so that he could remain in Springfield — and so Lincoln would not lose his doctor. Henry wrote specialists in Cincinnati about Lincoln. Lincoln wrote his partner Stuart and other congressmen, asking them to go the limit for Dr. Henry: "Unless he gets that job," said Lincoln, "he leaves Springfield; Dr. Henry is necessary to my existence."

The statements of his associates, and also his own, reveal a man suffering from a classical emotional depression. Ninian Edwards said he was "crazy as a loon," and James Conkling said that "he seems scarcely to possess strength enough to speak above a whisper."[36]

---

[36] This peculiar episode in Lincoln's life is recounted in William Herndon and Jesse Weik, *Herndon's Life of Lincoln*, pp. 69-71; Wilson and Davis, p. 592; Donald, pp. 86-88; Sandburg, Vol. 1, pp. 205-206.

BACKING DOWN

BY FEBRUARY HIS DEPRESSION was beginning to ease some. The romance with Mary Todd was in suspension, at best, but political events still interested him. The Democrats had won the state legislature and given offices and court appointments to their partisans. Douglas was made a Supreme Court judge. Lincoln assumed his usual outrage when the opposing party got power and took action that Lincoln wished he had himself been positioned to take. He expressed his outrage at length to Stuart. The Whigs formed a committee, with Lincoln as a member, which issued "An Appeal to the People of the State of Illinois," complaining of supposed Democratic attempts to subvert the judiciary's independence and undermine the rights of property and liberty of conscience. The irony of the accusation, as events would show, lay in Lincoln's future wartime disregard of rights.

The Legislature adjourned in March 1841. When he was 32, Lincoln's career in the Illinois legislature came to an end. He was tired of the legislature after four terms. He wasn't tired of politics; he remained a member of the Whig State Central Committee, the repository of the party's political power. He had become a skillful practitioner of the art of politics, an active floor leader for his party, a good public speaker, and a recognised hand at writing out the drafts of his party's bills. The law practice was good. Not so the state's financial condition. Illinois defaulted on its debt, dissolved the state bank, and terminated most of its internal improvements programs. Understandably, and not least on account of his innate ambition, Lincoln's attention began wandering to affairs outside Illinois. What about the U.S.

Congress was the question that more and more engaged his attention. To Speed he opened his mind. What had he done, he wished to know, to make people remember him?

During the spring of 1841 Mary Todd was being courted by another man, Edwin Webb, a widower with two children; but her thoughts were on Lincoln. She wrote Mercy Ann Levering, the future wife of Lincoln's fellow Whig James Conkling, saying that if Lincoln would again notice her, "much, much happiness would it afford me."

Lincoln and Stuart dissolved their partnership in April 1841. It had lasted four years. Lincoln needed a partner to attend to the business so that he could get out of the office to do what he liked — ride the circuit and politick, virtually one and the same activity. He found the right man in a new partner, Stephen T. Logan, a man of small stature and large ability. Logan was a lawyer's lawyer, capable, intelligent, informed on the law, diligent, assiduous, and accurate in attending to his duties. After practicing law in Kentucky for 10 years Logan had moved to Springfield, where he was a circuit court judge for two years. He then went into private practice. His hard work and ability earned him the reputation as the best lawyer in town. He was the perfect associate for a man of ambition such as Lincoln, whose deficiencies lay exactly in areas where Logan excelled. Office work did not attract Lincoln. His aims lay outside, in a broader field. But in the meantime he would partake of Logan's success and learn from his method.

The firm of Logan and Lincoln, busy and prosperous, had more cases before the Illinois Supreme Court than any other firm. Logan later called Lincoln "a pretty good lawyer." The practice helped Lincoln more than Logan, Lincoln learning firsthand from his partner the benefits accruing from careful preparation and detailed study of the facts and presentation before going into the courtroom.

In August 1841, Lincoln went to visit Joshua Speed, who had moved back to his parents' house in Kentucky. He had a delightful time. Speed was also anxious over the prospect of marriage. He was interested in a girl named Fanny Henning but had doubts similar to those Lincoln had entertained. Lincoln met Fanny, liked her, and encouraged Speed in his suit.

Speed went back to Springfield with Lincoln. On the river boat that was returning them they saw 12 slaves being transported. Lincoln wrote indignantly that the 12 were being sold "into perpetual slavery where the lash of the master is proverbially more ruthless and unrelenting than any other where." Yet to Lincoln the slaves seemed happier than anybody else on the boat, playing the fiddle, dancing, singing, joking, laughing, and playing cards: appearing to illustrate, as he saw it, the truth of the quotation, "'God tempers the wind to the shorn lamb,' or in other words, that He renders the worst of human conditions tolerable, while He permits the best to be nothing more than tolerable."

This referred as much to Lincoln's state of happiness as to theirs. He referred to the sight of those slaves years later as "a continual torment to me," saying that every time he touched the border of a slave state he saw something similar. Slavery "had the power of making me miserable."[37] Speed visited Lincoln until January 1842. Back home, he and Lincoln wrote each other. Lincoln's depression lifted as he and Speed discussed their mutual anxieties. Speed did marry Fanny Henning and wrote Lincoln of his great happiness. Lincoln began to think of Mary and regret his rejection of her.

Martin Van Buren wanted to be President again. Organising his campaign for the presidential election of 1844, he came to Illinois

---

[37] Beveridge, Vol. 1, p. 94.

in June 1842. The Democratic leaders of Springfield went to Rochester, six miles away to entertain him. Lincoln went along for the fun. The ex-president and the future president were the principle tavern performers, entertaining the politicians long into the night: two talented politicians practicing their trade, doing what they knew well how to do, namely, entertain a crowd and solicit support. Van Buren's anger because his party refused him the nomination in 1844 caused him to lead a schism within the Democratic party. This faction, with its rule-or-ruin attitude, later helped lift Lincoln to the presidency.

Lincoln, in the summer of 1842, began seeing Mary Ann Todd again. The necessities of courtship did not exclude the luxuries of his first and truest love, politics. Even romance was an adjunct to the interest in politics that absorbed him and consumed him.

Lincoln's career and personal life were prospering. Joshua Speed wrote Lincoln of the happiness of his own newly married life and urged his friend to follow suit. Lincoln and Mary were enjoying each other's company, as they always had.

Lincoln wrote on paper a detailed analysis of his political condition, showing how his political power was growing, and indicating where his future lay. To write down the facts of his ambition was the act of a man with a singular drive for power. Lincoln's career has been called a deed of charity. If it was public service he sought, he contrived again and again to achieve and embellish private ends.

On November 4, 1842, on a rainy afternoon, in Ninian Edward's house, Abraham Lincoln, age 33, and Mary Ann Todd, age 23, were married. Before the wedding, a boy, seeing Lincoln dressed in his formal clothes, asked him where he was going. Lincoln answered, "To Hell, I reckon." The statement revealed the man; it was a characteristic response: epigrammatic, succinct, with a touch of wit, but evasive of fact, vulgar in tone, and deliberately rude to the child.

Lincoln invited not a single member of his family to the wedding. Relatives learned of it only much later when Lincoln had traveled over to Coles County on business, dropped in for a short visit, and casually reported, "I am married now."

Mary and Lincoln enjoyed their life together, according to all evidence. They had pleasure in each other and in their Whig social connections. Not many husbands and wives are fortunate enough to enjoy the same subjects — to have so much in common. For a year they lived in a room at the Globe Tavern, where room and board cost them $4 a week. On August 1, 1843, their first child, Robert Todd, was born. A few months later they moved into a rented house, and then in January 1844, fourteen months after their wedding, they bought a substantial house for $1,200. They liked each other. Their marriage prospered.

The firm of Lincoln and Logan also prospered. Logan had a business-like nature. He filed his documents carefully; he attended to business promptly. He carefully thought out his cases and prepared them. He was thorough; he postponed nothing. Some people considered him the best lawyer in the state.

Lincoln was an opposite type — a courthouse performer, good at swaying juries, though far less concerned about facts than was his partner. Unlike Logan, Lincoln was careless and forgetful, admitting to neglect and procrastination, to putting business routine aside and turning his mind to things more pleasant. He clowned a bit in the courtroom and in public. He liked "monkeyshines," practiced mimicry and parody. He was the chief storyteller on the circuit.

Lincoln liked politics more than law. Whereas he would avoid business routine, he would study politics with great intensity. He spent days studying the tariff issue, and for practice was willing to speak anywhere on the subject. As was his custom, he was highly partisan on the tariff issue. He would debate free trade advocates anywhere.

He was a classic Northern Whig (subsequently Republican): abolitionist (though never unwise enough to reveal it), pro-high tariff, pro-internal improvements, pro-national bank, unfriendly to the South, an opponent of Texas annexation.

In February 1842, the Illinois state auditor, James Shields, acting in his capacity as a government officer, refused to permit taxes to be paid in the worthless notes of the bankrupt state bank. The bank had become insolvent because of legislative actions which Lincoln had led. Lincoln was chief and loudest of the Whigs who had put across the pledging of the state's credit to finance vast public works (internal improvements), in effect creating money where none existed. That Lincoln, no great hand at personal money management, would have the capacity to help manage the finances of an entire state was too much to expect. His derelictions contributed to Illinois' financial distress, including default on its bonds. Not only the individual bondholders but the state bank itself held worthless paper. In the private realm this state of affair is often condemned as fraud; under government — that is, public — sponsorship, the matter takes on a different cast. Blame is hard to fix. Who did it? Who can be held to account? Can anyone in particular? Maybe, and, again, maybe not.

The Illinois State Bank had found its paper worthless. "Easy money" had become worthless money. Lincoln wanted the bank to continue creating money to subsidize the various government-paid projects of public works. Shields was trying to save the state by preserving its solvency in the monetary crisis.

Lincoln went to his trustiest tool — his pen. He is alleged to have written letters attacking Shields. These he took to his friend Simeon Francis, whose Whig newspaper, *the Sangamon Journal*, began publishing letters signed "Rebecca," adopting the persona of a shrewd, crude countrywoman. Mary and a girlfriend had a hand in the project, but the director was Lincoln. The letters mercilessly ridiculed Shields in the context of assailing Democratic financial policies. Lincoln might have intended his anonymous sallies to stand as a splendid piece of fun, but their language — "conceited dunce" was an example — bit deeply.

Shields charged into the *Journal*'s office of the editor, Lincoln's friend Francis, and demanded to know who wrote the letters. The responsibility, he learned, was Lincoln's. Shields, a bachelor Irishman of approximately Lincoln's own age, wrote to "require a full, positive, and absolute retraction of all offensive allusions used by you in these offensive communications, in relation to my private character and standing as a man, as an apology for the insults conveyed in them." The implication was clear: A duel — though illegal in Illinois — was in the offing.

Lincoln asked Albert Taylor Bledsoe, a local lawyer and West Point graduate, to train him in the use of the broadsword. (Bledsoe later served in the Confederate government and wrote books in defense of slavery and secession.) Challenger and challenged met on a sandbar on the Mississippi River, in Missouri jurisdiction, prepared to battle it out with the broadswords that Lincoln had identified as the weapon of choice. Discussion ensued among seconds and lawyers. Lincoln affirmed that he had meant no affront to "the personal or private character of Mr. Shields as a gentleman or a man." The two shook hands, returning to shore in a rowboat. Carl Sandburg, in his fantasy biography of Lincoln, claimed that "Lincoln and Shields came off the boat together, in easy and pleasant chat."[38]

The incident curbed whatever taste for serious invective Lincoln might have harboured. Henceforth defamation was phrased in careful manner, and in a style that increasingly took on a moralistic tone of wounded dignity, but that was still partisan, political, and simply not factual. Lincoln had a way, cruel as ever, of describing an opponent and his words in a way that was not correctly to be inferred from the man's career or statements but was not obviously defamatory. He had no intention of hurling a missile that could ricochet back upon himself. James Shields's challenge shook Lincoln to his marrow. "The episode," says David Donald, "remained one of Lincoln's most painful memories" — not least due to "the realization that he had allowed himself to be ruled by his turbulent emotions."[39]

Some historians have tried to lay the blame for this imbroglio upon Mary for supposedly inciting a duel that was clearly Lincoln's own affair. It was Lincoln who made the charges, who tried to evade the challenge, who recanted finally his accusations. The Lincoln canonists, elevating him to sainthood, have had sometimes to diminish those around him. Mary Todd was blamed for inciting the duel and for inciting him to power. The truth is, Lincoln's ambition arose from the springs of his own soul; it was not his wife who drove him but his own inner fires. He led, she followed.

Nobody ever led Lincoln — not his father, his peers, his law partners, his political group, his cabinet, or his generals. Only his ambitions governed. Whatever the circumstances, he led, he

---

[38] Sandburg, Vol. 1, p. 283.
[39] Donald, p. 93.

decided, he controlled. He might cover his designs, he might trim his sails to the public wind, but he never changed his course. Partisan Republican history has called Mrs. Lincoln a scheming, ambitious Lady Macbeth; insane; a total burden on the man and on his career. This is another myth. She was certainly less scheming in marrying him than he in marrying her. At the time of their marriage she had the better of the two in assets social and financial. She is called a further thorn in the crown of martyrdom of Abraham Lincoln. History has criticized her for her ambition for her husband, but not him for his ambition for himself.

Mary Todd was a desirable helpmate to Lincoln for many reasons. She was an attractive woman, comfortably fixed and socially prominent, with powerful Whig connections and a pleasing personality. She was good company to Lincoln, interested in and able to discuss popular subjects of the day. Her personal and public qualities were attractive to him. Whether or not (taking Ann Rutledge into account) Mary was Lincoln's first love, she shared enthusiastically in his great passion of politics. He stayed involved in politics continuously. He never left it off.

A Thirst for Distinction

FROM 1841 TO 1846, LINCOLN worked hard for the Whig nomination to Congress. He spoke often, drawing on scriptural authority (in a selective way, of course) to urge the party fellows to remain united. The Gospels of Matthew and Mark report Jesus's confirmation of the truth that "A house divided against itself cannot stand." He declared, in complementary fashion, that "Union is strength" — a declaration as old as Aesop. His candidacy was no secondary activity; it was his principal interest. Many long letters, still extant, attest to the devotion, time, and effort he gave to his ambition.

In the spring of every odd-numbered year, as irresistibly as the force that sends green shoots bursting from the ground, Lincoln reached out for political increase. It is in the odd year that the party candidate must begin the campaign to gain his party's nomination for the even year. In 1841 Lincoln had grown tired of the state legislature and set his sights on the U.S. Congress. He confessed to a friend he would very much like to go Congress. But in 1843 a Whig district convention chose as its candidate the capable and popular John J. Hardin. Lincoln discerned an opening for himself, nevertheless. He persuaded the convention to anoint Edward D. Baker, an English immigrant, for the nomination in 1844. The decision had two consequences: It signaled Hardin that he should clear the way for Baker; and it suggested the same course to Baker when his own time should run out. Who would be left to run then but Abraham Lincoln, indefatigable Whig strategist? And so it came to pass.

Hardin briefly got in the way by mulling another campaign for Congress, but Lincoln disposed of his hopes before the convention. Hardin joined the army in order to lead Illinois volunteers in the Mexican War. He was killed at the battle of Buena Vista (where Jefferson Davis was wounded and celebrated for his courage and skill). Lincoln finally obtained realisation of his congressional ambition in 1846, defeating the Democrat Peter Cartwright, a Methodist circuit rider. Lincoln was already altering the Whig way of doing business. He saw nomination by convention as better than loose, uncoordinated campaigning by a multiplicity of candidates. He urged that the Whigs to stop fighting among themselves for the sake of that unity he would so strongly commend to the whole nation in due course.

For all his obvious value to the Whigs, Lincoln was something less than the party's Galahad. His intra-party struggles had given rise to singular charges concerning such a man of the people as he presented himself to be. He heard himself described within his own party as the "candidate of pride, wealth, and aristocratic family distinction." That such a description, even as campaign rhetoric, could be employed against him shows that Lincoln was not even at this early period of his career regarded as the humble figure that he and his faction later tried to present to the public.

He was also labeled an infidel and a deist. He belonged to and attended no church. Lincoln's own Sangamon County Whig delegation had given its vote to Baker in 1843. As a member of the county delegation Lincoln was honour-bound to vote for Baker, but he had not promised to quit campaigning. Stymied by Sangamon County's defection, yet hungry for the nomination, Lincoln went to Menard County, winning its delegates' support so that he would be introduced in case Baker and Hardin should tie at the convention. They did not, as it turned out. Hardin and Baker were apparently on good terms with each other throughout the affair; not so with Lincoln.

The election of 1844 had found Lincoln honing his rhetorical skills on that which was called, literally and properly, "the stump." He went into Indiana addressing rallies for Henry Clay, who was running against the Democrat James K. Polk, a champion of national expansion. In Illinois nobody did more party work for the Whigs than Lincoln, but in the end, Polk took Illinois, Indiana, and 170 electoral votes to the Whigs' 105. One ominous note indicating what was to come was that James G. Birney, running on the antislavery Liberty Party ticket, won 62,000 votes. Polk's popular margin over Clay was less than that number.

Lincoln took no particular interest in the abolitionist efforts against newly independent Texas joining the Union. As tensions multiplied with Mexico over American interest in Mexican-owned California as well as Texas, his speeches failed to contradict the general popular sentiment of support for U.S. expansion. He made no statement hostile to the Mexican War — which had begun in 1846 — until he arrived in Congress and joined the partisan Whig effort to discredit the Democrats who had initiated the war. His lifelong practice, after all, had been to search for issues useful in advancing his political prospects. In due course, slavery would serve that purpose with a grandeur impossible to predict more than a decade before the initiation of war between South and North.

Shortly after the 1844 presidential election, Lincoln had ended his partnership with Logan. Their career interests were different. Logan was a lawyer; Lincoln, though a member of the Bar, was primarily a politician. There was stress between them. Lincoln had reached a higher rung in his climb. What Logan had to give had been received. Now Lincoln needed a new kind of partner.

William Herndon had read law with Lincoln and Logan and was ready to begin practice. He had lived with Lincoln and Joshua

Speed at Speed's store. After the disagreement with Logan, Lincoln decided to leave and start his own firm. He asked Herndon to be his partner. Herndon eagerly accepted. In Herndon Lincoln found the perfect mate.

There were many reasons why. Herndon was 11 years younger than Lincoln: literary, well-informed, a diligent student who could supply Lincoln with facts on any subject, intensely interested in contemporary social and political affairs. Their politics were similar. Lincoln, pro-business, with a bias toward expediency, believed in the interventions of that which we nowadays call big government. Neither was religious after a traditional Christian fashion. They were disciples, rather, of contemporary secular social dogma, the great idea of their time in place of religion.

Herndon, a zealous abolitionist, agreed with Lincoln on the slavery question. Moreover, he was a loyal political agent, who diligently did yeoman work in support of his partner. To Lincoln, Herndon's greatest asset was a nature which made him glad to accept the role of inferior in the firm, a status neither Stuart nor Logan would have accepted. Herndon always called his partner "Mr. Lincoln." Lincoln liked that; he was quick to adopt the role of superior in rank, however much he wore the humble air in public. He had people call him "Mr. Lincoln." No "Honest Abe" was he, with the implications of familiarity the term carried. (Various narratives, none of impeccable origin, trace the famous nickname to supposed episodes in Lincoln's youth.) Certain it is that the Republican Party saw advantage in popularizing use of the name, and belief in its premises.) Lincoln for his part called Herndon "Billy."

During their association Herndon reportedly was better read, but Lincoln was better "said." Herndon reported hearing Lincoln relate the same story three times in as many hours. Their operation featured Herndon in the background, running the office; Lincoln in the forefront, running for office. Finally, Herndon was a member of the Young Whigs group, extroverted and hard-drinking, a useful link to youthful active newcomers in politics. It was another group Lincoln would enlist in his service, and Herndon would be his recruiting sergeant.

William Herndon was an example of the grande idée — the great idea, whether right or wrong, that can unite a people. He was more intellectual than Lincoln, but their philosophies were the same, differing only in that Lincoln tempered his to serve his ambition. To judge from the record, he spoke less often from the heart than from consideration of the effects his words would make upon a given audience.

He learned, as we have seen, to blend Scripture with worldly wisdom. Consider the Whig pamphlet whose chief author he was, and the terms in which he spoke of unity, saying "That union is strength, is a truth that has been known, illustrated and declared in various ways and forms in all ages of the world. That great fabulist and philosopher Aesop illustrated it by his fable of the bundle of sticks; and he whose wisdom surpasses that of all the philosophers [note the sideways reference to Jesus, proclaimed in Scripture as Son of God] has declared that 'A house divided against itself cannot stand.'" Lincoln was raised on the Bible. The few books he read as a youth were good ones. Their lessons were classical, the allusions familiar. For use as high-sounding abstractions they were unsurpassed. He was to use the phrase "a house divided" several times, and finally again with frightening effect and devastating result. A phrase he carried with him for use in any need, was taken literally and became self-fulfilling.

The transparently political side of Lincoln's nature is on view in his determined quest for a seat in Congress. We have noted already some of his maneuvers to secure the Whig nomination for the House of Representatives. Letters from the period show the most exhausting devotion of time and detail to that end. John J. Hardin, as we have seen, had been elected to Congress in 1842 before standing aside for Edward Baker in 1844. Lincoln had tried so hard to pre-empt Baker in the pre-election maneuvering in 1843 that it is likely that Baker felt ill will toward him. He never ceased fighting Baker until forced to do so.

A considerable irony, in view of such considerations, was that, Lincoln's second son, born in 1846, received in baptism the name of Edward, in honour of his rival. This, notwithstanding that the two men were not close. Two sons had now been born to Lincoln. Not yet had he been able to act on his promise to name a child for his benefactor Joshua Speed. Speed was now permanently off the scene; Lincoln needed him no more; his early benefactions to Lincoln had been consumed. The first child was named for Mary's father, Robert Todd. Now, perhaps Edward Baker would succumb to the same brand of flattery. Lincoln needed him in 1846 because a collaboration of Baker with Hardin would eliminate Lincoln's candidacy.

In opposing Hardin, Lincoln ran a far more sophisticated campaign than he ever had done. He needed no more instruction than that furnished so clearly by James Shields. Lincoln said nothing derogatory about Hardin. He began working earlier than Hardin. He lined up newspaper editors in his district before Hardin could act. He had his partisans spread the word that Hardin was not going to run for Congress but, rather, for the governorship. At the same time, he warned his agents to be sure that his name was not associated with the subterfuge. Further, he allowed it to be claimed that at Pekin in 1843 Hardin had agreed to avoid conflict not only with Baker, but with Lincoln also. That agreement seems never to have occurred. Lincoln solicited the Whig delegates before Hardin did.

Careful to say nothing offensive about his rival, adopting for the first time the lofty, moralistic, superior manner that became his trademark, Lincoln was able to demean Hardin's candidacy without demeaning Hardin. It was skillful work, well done. Hardin had started too late; he withdrew in February 1846. Lincoln was nominated by acclamation at the district convention in Petersburg.

The off-year election of 1846 was fought on the issues of the tariff and internal improvements. The Whigs were as usual for high tariffs and heavy spending of general government funds on local public works. Opponents regarded both policies as no more than disguised patronage, benefiting the few at the expense of the many. The Democrats were the party of smaller government, but gradually Northern Democrats were beginning to like the idea of getting government money for projects which benefited them. Polk, a Southern Democrat, had refused to approve such spending. Polk's nomination had angered the former Democratic president Martin Van Buren of New York, whose faction resented its elimination. Purely political rivalry began the split of Northern and Southern Democrats, a factor disastrous for the party and nation in 1860.

The dispute with Mexico broke into war during the campaign. Lincoln's campaign statements, as we have seen, were in agreement with the general pro-Texas, anti-Mexican feelings. Illinois volunteers flocked to join the army bound for Mexico. Two of them were Lincoln's predecessors in Congress, Hardin and Baker. Hardin was to die there. Had he survived his wound at Buena Vista and returned home, he might have become too big a figure for Lincoln's ambitions to deflect by another tactic of "rotation." Alive, Hardin might have made Lincoln politically dead. Lincoln's ambition had a later effect upon Edward Baker.

The Democratic candidate, Peter Cartwright, ran a poor campaign against Lincoln, in the strongest Whig district in Illinois. His credentials as a celebrated Methodist preacher inspired, if futilely, the characterization of Lincoln as deist and infidel but permitted Lincoln, in a handbill, to brush aside the charge with affirmation of belief in a Supreme Being, and in the truth of the Scriptures. In fact, Lincoln was a secular moralist. His use of Scripture was political, idiomatic, illustrative, metaphysical, given the tenuous nature of his attachment to Christianity. James Matheny, a Springfield friend, said he had heard Lincoln "call Christ a bastard." To John Stuart his unorthodoxy "bordered on atheism."[40] In this campaign he got a Sunday School lesson: atheists are not successful politicians. From this time forward the Bible idiom became Lincoln's vocabulary.

Lincoln was elected to Congress on August 3, 1846. He wrote to Speed what he felt so often after election to a higher seat of power, that his election to Congress had pleased him less than he had supposed it would. The gratification of ambition seems never to have satisfied him fully.

Not until the following year would the 30th Congress convene. During that interim, Lincoln never stopped politicking. He traveled to Chicago to the "River and Harbor Convention," a Whig meeting illustrative of the real force dividing North and South economies. Almost all the attendees were Northern politicians and business representatives, joined as a lobby group

---

[40] Richard Carwardine, *Lincoln: A Life of Purpose and Power*, Knopf, 2006, p. 3.

for government money (internal improvements) to subsidize their business. Nowhere did the Constitution authorise the spending of federal money to subsidize various economic groups, but the lure of such largesse was too great for various interests to resist trying to get it. At this meeting there was hardly a Southerner present. The Southerners were not Lincoln's constituency. Lincoln met the people he wanted to meet, among them Horace Greeley, editor of the *New York Tribune,* and Thurlow Weed, boss of the Whig party in New York. He met other powerful business and political figures.

This group was almost a cabal of interests which wanted to use federal government power for their own benefit, assuming the South could be levered out of the way. The trail of these men's doings at the convention led directly to the batteries of Charleston Harbor and the bloody stream of Bull Run.

Lincoln knew that these two issues, internal improvements and the tariff — both of them methods of using federal power to benefit Northern economic interests — were too important for those interests to let die. It was this group, united by mutual desire for public money to enhance private profit, that became the backbone of the Republican Party. Slavery was not mentioned in the party's early annals. Neither the Republican Party nor the war it started can be laid at the doorstep of the black man. He had nothing to do with either. He was only an excuse. Behind both issues was the power drive of white men. The attendees at this convention were powerful political and economic figures. Out of their outrage at Polk and the Democrats for opposing government spending to benefit their interests was born the Republican Party.

Lincoln studied the tariff and practiced his arguments for it. He never sat back in any crowd, nor would he do so in Congress. When he got there, he wanted to be ready to talk. The subjects he studied were the prominent issues presented to Congress. He readied his speeches before he entered the doors of Congress.

After months of anticipation, finally the time came to go to Washington, D.C. En route, the Lincolns, with 4-year-old Bob and 18-month-old Ed in tow, stopped in Lexington, Kentucky, to visit the Todds. Lincoln attended a Whig rally, heard his idol Henry Clay condemn the war with Mexico, declared by Congress May 13, 1846, after Mexican troops crossed the Rio Grande and attacked a unit of U.S. soldiers. "[W]ar exists by the act of Mexico herself," President Polk had declared. Lincoln, who had run for office voicing support for the country's general position in favour of territorial expansion, promptly adopted the national Whig position. Leading Whigs had no intention of endorsing Democrat Polk's actions, and Lincoln had no intention of opposing his party.

A One-Term Congressman

WHEN LINCOLN TOOK HIS SEAT March 4, 1847, he was the lone Whig from Illinois. Washington was a quiet Southern town of 34,000 people. The operation of the entire federal government cost but $60 million a year. Government debt was negligible. Lincoln, as usual, was operating on borrowed money. Senator Stephen Douglas, the man Lincoln was to accuse of a variety of sins, was another of Lincoln's timely benefactors, telling him upon his arrival to charge his bills to him. Lincoln accepted and made use of Douglas's credit. The Lincolns took up residence at Mrs. Sprigg's boarding house, known as the "Abolition House." It was the headquarters of the "Free-Soil" anti-South Whigs.

He became close friends with Joshua R. Giddings, the violent slavery-hating congressman from Ohio — censured once by his colleagues for intemperate language but triumphantly returned to the House by his constituents. The two men shared an anti-slavery worldview, but Giddings tended to express himself in over-heated language. Lincoln's views were shared in private and muted in public. The two were harmonious in philosophy. They reinforced each other's views, agreed in politics, enjoyed each other's company. On December 21, 1847, Giddings presented a petition to forbid slave-trading in the District of Columbia. Lincoln voted for it.

Lincoln quickly gained his usual pace as chief story-teller and was popular at all social gatherings. He never departed from his axiom, "You catch more flies with honey than with gall."

Lincoln was indefatigable in political activities. In Congress he was impressed — somewhat paradoxically, given the great divergence of the two men's philosophies — by the dignified personality of John C. Calhoun of South Carolina, profound political thinker, twice vice president, and defender of states' rights as well as slavery. When it came to oratory, Lincoln fell short not only of the great Webster but of numerous lesser aspirants to greatness. He could be shrill and dogmatic. He did not overcome his defects immediately, but he studied the calm, reserved manner of Calhoun, "the Great Nullifier," and emerged from the Congress having moderated his own style. He began to conceal demagogic ideas in a dark rhetorical cloak.

The Whigs were united against Polk chiefly because he had vetoed two internal improvements bills on grounds that the government enjoyed no constitutional power to finance such projects. The Mexican War — a conflict, in their worldview, originated by the "slaveocracy" for its own benefit — fanned the flames of their animosity toward Polk and the Democrats. A Chicago newspaper described the vetoes as evidence of a Southern coup. Slavery could be used anywhere to indict the enemy party, the Democrats. Lincoln, in 1847 and 1848, voted consistently for intruding the federal government into the slavery issue. On January 19, 1848, he voted for a protective tariff. On January 31, 1848, he voted to prohibit slave ownership in the District of Columbia. When written, the Constitution was regarded as having excluded slavery from federal power, reserving oversight of that institution to the states.

By the time Lincoln took his seat in Congress, the war with Mexico was half finished. Its conclusion, with the Treaty of Guadalupe-Hidalgo, February 2, 1848, would cede California and New Mexico to the United States and acknowledge the Rio Grande border of Texas. The Whigs did not want the territory taken in as states because the new states would be Democratic. The Southern people, like the Northern, wanted new lands for settlement. They had their capital invested in slaves. If they could not take their slaves into the new areas, then they could not go there themselves. The Northern Democrats for the most part either failed to care or sided with the South. The power drive, man's besetting sin, was at work. The Northern internal improvements and tariff interests did not welcome any additional "small government" states. If additional congressman were to come to Washington they must be internal improvement and tariff men.

Non-clarity of motive — a constant factor in the affairs of mankind, in particular the political affairs — has obscured the principal political operations of the period. Was concern for the persons of slaves the main factor at work here? Or was the matter more devious? Were Northern whites more concerned with power for themselves than with power for Southern blacks? Good reason exists to affirm the latter.

Consider the case of Congressman Jacob Brinkerhoff of Ohio, a Van Buren Democrat, rebuffed by the Polk administration in his quest for political offices for his friends at home. Not liking this Southern president to begin with, Brinkerhoff collaborated with another Northern Democrat, Congressman David Wilmot of Pennsylvania, in a measure to put a spoke in the president's rapidly moving wheel. As a Polk opponent, Brinkerhoff knew that any bill he introduced would attract attention, so he decided on a subterfuge. He induced the less-visible Wilmot to attach a proviso to an important $2 million appropriations bill meant to facilitate negotiations with Mexico for territorial adjustments. The so-called Wilmot Proviso passed the House before its opponents knew of it. It provided that any new territory that came into the United States from the Mexican War treaty should be free — not slave territory. The Proviso passed twice in the House and was defeated in the Senate. Its backers put it repeatedly as an amendment to virtually every bill introduced. Lincoln said he voted "aye" for the Wilmot Proviso "as good as forty times."[41]

Whigs fought the annexation of any Mexican territory that might be formed into additional pro-Southern slave states. The other party had dominated politics since 1800; the Whigs wanted no more Democratic states. A bitter partisan fight broke out, and Lincoln outdid his Whig allies in heaping abuse on the Democrats. Behind the war he saw politics and took a position the exact opposite of his stance in 1861. In December 1847 and January 1848, he demanded that President Polk specify the "particular spot of soil on which" fighting broke out between U.S. and Mexican troops disputing the borders of Texas. Lincoln accused Polk of starting the war to save himself from public scrutiny by the ancient device of war, by "fixing the public gaze on military glory." He called Polk "a bewildered, confounded, miserably perplexed man," whose mind was "taxed beyond its power."[42]

James Knox Polk manifested the classic principles of the Democratic Party. He was strongly in favour of annexation of Texas and of a plain, small, and economical central government. He came into office promising to fulfill his principles: not to seek re-election; rather, to limit government, settle the boundary disputes with Britain and Mexico, establish an independent treasury, reduce the tariff, and reduce the need for taxes. He did them all.

---

[41] *Lincoln, A Documentary Portrait*, p. 83.
[42] Lincoln, *Speeches and Writings*, Vol. 1, p. 171.

In both personality and principles he was opposite to Lincoln: retiring, not social; quiet, not a talker; sincere, not calculating; inhibiting himself and government when he became the government. Before he was elected, he stated clearly his principles and platform.

Posterity increasingly calls Polk one of America's best presidents, the only one to announce what he wanted to do, and then do it. Lincoln's opposition to him was based on party affiliation alone. It is impossible to find principle in Lincoln's opposition to the war — only politics. Contrast his hatred of the war with Mexico with his eagerness for war on the South. The very words he used against Polk, saying Polk had no reason to fight Mexico in 1847, were much more applicable to his invasion of the South in 1861. In the Mexican conflict, the adversaries had been fighting over territory for more than a decade. Hundreds of people had been killed. No such events had occurred in 1861. The war Lincoln opposed was all politics to him, just as the war he started would be for politics. He saw every phenomenon as politics. He called the Mexican War both unnecessary and unconstitutional. Ironically, the charge could more honestly be levied against Lincoln in 1861 than against Polk in 1848.

Let the president, he said, invade a neighbouring nation "and you allow him to make war at pleasure."[43] Lincoln's escape clause, to be sure, was that in his view the states making up the Confederacy lacked standing as a "nation."

Lincoln spoke at length, and at ease by his own statement, in the House just as he did in Springfield. On the floor of Congress, on January 13, 1848, he declared his belief that people had a right to revolution. "Any people anywhere being inclined and having the

---

[43] Lincoln, A *Documentary Portrait*, p. 59.

power have the right to rise up and shake off the existing government, and form a new one that suits them better. This is a most valuable, a most sacred right — a right which we hope and believe is to liberate the world. Nor is this right confined to cases in which the whole people of an existing government may choose to exercise it. ... Any portion of such people that can, may revolutionize and make their own of so much of the territory as they inhabit."[44] The right that Lincoln had proclaimed in 1848 he denied in 1860, because politically it would have killed his party and thus his career.

Even the worshipful Herndon wrote Lincoln that his assaults on Polk went too far. The Whigs had managed to get through Congress by one vote a resolution thanking the officers of the Mexican War, but including the clause, "in a war unnecessarily and unconstitutionally begun by the President of the United States." Even Herndon opposed that statement. But Lincoln was ever seeking an issue to "view with alarm" to inflame an audience, to enlist a following.

And there was, during his term in Congress, simply no other issue. Lincoln took the only one available. In the North the Whig faction did not want more territory to form states to send more Democratic politicians to Washington. There was always a group that opposed any enlargement of the South and contiguous areas with agricultural economies. The group had fought the Louisiana Purchase, admission of Missouri to the Union, and more recently acquisition of the former Mexican territories of the Southwest. This was Lincoln's only issue. He jumped for it and fell.

Nonetheless, Polk was correct: if the United States had committed aggression in physically contesting Mexico's claim to

---

[44] Lincoln, *Speeches and Writings*, p. 167.

Texas land north of the Nueces River, so had Mexico injured the rights and lives of Americans in suppressing the claims of American settlers for primacy in Texas and in crossing the Rio Grande to attack American soldiers. Lincoln had criticized Polk for invading a nation that had invaded his own. Later on, Lincoln invaded the Southern Confederacy, a nation which nobody accused of wanting to invade Lincoln's, desiring only to be rid of allegiance to it.

Lincoln argued that the Congress only, not the President, possessed the power of making war. In fact, Congress did approve war against Mexico by votes of 40 to 2 in the Senate and 170 to 14 in the House. Not until July 1861 — three months after the start of hostilities between North and South — did Congress convene. By then, Lincoln had called up 75,000 three-month volunteers and suspended habeas corpus in Maryland to prevent that state's secession. Congress, in the face of accomplished actions, acquiesced. Lincoln had learned a lesson: a leader needs an excuse to start a war. Once the war begins, the advantage is his.

Lincoln worried, given Herndon's disapproval of his position, what the people back home, the voters, must be thinking. The *Belleville Advocate* reported that in Clark County a meeting of Whigs and Democrats had adopted a resolution praying that his constituents might "cease to remember him, except to rebuke him."[45] The Whigs of his district refused to nominate him for a second term.

Lincoln was ignored in Congress, but in Illinois his fierce attacks on the Mexican War were equated with betrayal of his country and of constituents who were fighting for that country. While

---

[45] Sandburg, p. 372.

Lincoln was castigating the President and, by implication, encouraging the enemy, one of his predecessors in the seat he held — Edward Baker — was fighting in Mexico. His other predecessor, John Hardin, was dying there.

As many of his constituents noted, in Congress he was merely another new member, obtrusive but ignored. But politically he was never still. He wrote dozens of letters daily supporting his political future — "fixing fences."

Soon after he arrived in Washington, Lincoln, with five other Whigs, had organized the Taylor Club — named for "Old Rough and Ready," otherwise known as Gen. Zachary Taylor, a Whig and hero of the war. Just as Lincoln would use disapproval of the war as a measure to gain attention, so he would use approval of Taylor to the same end. He knew that Taylor would be a presidential candidate no Democrat could beat. Thus Lincoln went to work trying to arrange Taylor's nomination. Lincoln was busy with his pen and personality toward this effort. During his entire one-term sojourn in Washington Lincoln worked for his political party.

The most notable member of the Taylor Club was a man Lincoln called his friend, Alexander H. Stephens, then a Whig congressman from Georgia, destined to become vice president of the Confederate States of America. Lincoln had nothing but praise for Stephens, who opposed the Mexican War at the same time he defended slavery's introduction into the new territories. Nonetheless, Lincoln's party and his career came first with him. As president, he rejected coldly all Stephens's efforts for reconciliation in 1860-61.

In March 1848 Mary and the children returned home. Lincoln finished his term alone. In June he went as a delegate to the Whig party convention in Philadelphia. He worked for the nomination of Taylor, predicting the general could not be beaten. He liked Clay, but preferred a winner.

In July in Congress he spoke against General Lewis Cass, of Michigan, veteran of the War of 1812, onetime Secretary of War, and now Democratic nominee for president. The speech was humorous, but vulgar — a nonfactual lampoon.[46] Lincoln was humble only when it was useful to appear so. He spoke at length on the fact that General Cass had billed the federal government for cost of rations for himself and staff: $730 in a year. This, from a congressman whose two weeks of travel between Springfield and Washington, D.C., had so recently cost the government $1830! Lincoln castigated Cass for altering his stand on issues, another sport with which Lincoln was not personally unfamiliar. He operated as a voice of whatever position best served him. His family's absence left him more time for politicking. All his reading and studying, and most of his time were spent to that end. He wrote dozens of letters each day promoting his political career.

---

[46] Donald, p. 129.

OBSTRUCTIVE BUT UNNOTICED

THE WHIGS, WITH TAYLOR at the top of their ticket, won nationally in 1848. Lincoln had worked hard for his party. The principle of national party prominence acting as barrier to the presidency was operative once more. Clay and Webster, the Whig leaders, dominated their party, but their party would not nominate them as neither could have won the election. (The same factor would allow Lincoln to win nomination in 1860 over the better-known Republicans Seward and Chase.) Zachary Taylor, a hero of the fighting in Mexico, was the logical choice. Lincoln, ever the politician, approved. Victory and power, not principle, were always Lincoln's primary interests. His opposition to slavery did not impede approval of a slaveholder — Taylor — as president.

The Whigs were dividing into two factions. One group, truly national in outlook, wanted to contrive a policy of presenting candidates who could win support from every state. The members of this group had seen over and over again that the sectional and divisive philosophy that lay at the core of the Northern Whig faction would not win. It alarmed too many voters. The Whigs had won with Harrison and John Tyler of Virginia, but had lost with Clay against Polk. They had won once again with the mild, honest, and non-partisan Taylor at their head.

The New England Whigs were gaining strength. They were a faction both politically and economically hostile to the South, following the precedent of the Federalists. The essential Whig philosophy was at variance with that of Taylor, whose only claim to fame was victory in a war they and Lincoln had bitterly denounced as unnecessary and unjust. Furthermore, they called the war a slave owners' conspiracy. How could Whigs be asked to vote for a man who was a big slaveowner?

There was danger that many Whigs, especially the New England variety, would join the new "Free Soil" party, formed by Van Buren's Northern Democratic faction after the rejection of their hero in favour of Polk in 1844. The Van Buren faction, known as the Barnburners, had sat in the power seats a long time: two terms with Jackson and one with the canny "Sage of Kinderhook," Van Buren himself. Polk's nomination had given victory to the Democrats but had wrested power from the Van Buren faction. The Barnburners wanted to punish the Southern Democrats who had successfully sponsored Polk. This Northern group of professional politicians represented the business interests who wanted federal taxes to subsidize their commerce and industry (internal improvements), and who feared the balance between slave and free states would be tipped by admission to the Union of states carved from the territories. This little-noticed split set the stage for the realignment of power that brought on the Civil War and demonstrates irrefutably that politics really is the struggle for power. Now there were Democrats motivated to injure fellow Democrats, prepared to rebuke the strong Southern states by calling them habitats of the "slaveocracy."

Unfortunately for the Union, there existed in much of the North an inherent hatred for the South that was as old as the Union itself. This dislike was deep and ingrained in the Northern Democrats, as it had been also among the Federalists. Free Soil party candidates were strong. Van Buren was nominated for the presidency. He had been the leader of the inner-core Northern Democrat professionals for over a decade. Charles Francis Adams, nominated for vice president, was the son of John Quincy Adams, who had spent 20 years in the House of Representatives opposing the South. Adams repeatedly introduced into Congress anti-slavery resolutions. The Adamses disliked Southerners, from Jefferson forward, being themselves of the Federalist and Whig persuasion. Van Buren was, of course, a Democrat. The affiliation of these two Northern factions was an evil event for the South. Shifting power vectors were pointing their arrows southward. The commercial and manufacturing interests were fast growing in the North. They wanted high tariffs (paid for by the agricultural South) to provide money for the internal improvements they saw as propelling the country — and the capitalist class — forward.

It was the mutual self-interest of these formerly separate, now united, party factions that would precipitate war against the South. Northern factory owners sought the combination of cheap raw materials and a ready and profitable market. The South, on the other hand, wanted to be allowed to continue the trade begun in the 1600's with European nations. Every river in the South was a highway to Europe, sending agricultural products and bringing cheaper and better manufactured goods than the North's fledgling industry could so far provide. The tariff changed that balance, making European goods too expensive to compete with Northern wares.

Power was the goal of the North. The Free Soil party drew its membership from Northern monied and political interests seeking advantage over the South. Its leaders were motivated additionally by the desire for an issue that would ratify and establish their power. Fearing loss of their own members, the Whigs made it their business to see that the Free Soil party did more harm to the Democrats than to themselves. They worked to keep the Free Soilers from enticing away Whigs, and to use the Free Soil doctrine to injure the Democrats. This was the kind of work Lincoln could do well. Thus, the Whigs were forced to take up anti-slavery positions.

In September 1848, Lincoln travelled New England to speak for the Whig ticket. He spoke at both Cambridge and Lowell, in Massachusetts. At Worcester he was introduced by his distant cousin, the state's ex-governor Levi Lincoln. The representative of the Illinois Lincolns told the state Whig Convention there that he and his constituents felt modest compared to the New England people and that he considered the Eastern men "instructed and wise." Concerning slavery, he said the people of Illinois believed as did the people of Massachusetts except perhaps they did not speak so constantly about it., which was not exactly true. He spoke the views held by his audience, which in this case was made up chiefly of abolitionists. He was well received. Lincoln was after all a gifted actor, affecting a style natural — "offhand and familiar."

At Cambridge he followed the speech of William H. Seward, former governor of New York and, at the time, six weeks away from becoming a U.S. senator. (Seward called Lincoln's offering "a rambling storyteller speech, putting the audience in good humour, but avoiding any extended discussion of the slavery question.") Seward blamed the Southern opposition to "Internal Improvements" on slavery. As he told it, "the party of slavery" — meaning the party not his own — opposed improvements to internal trade, because railroads, rivers, and canals were highways for the escape of bondsmen. The party of liberty — the Seward-Lincoln party — by contrast would cover the country with railroads and canals to promote general happiness, binding the people with "the bonds of interest and affection." A demagogic, untrue, and silly statement it certainly was. It bore one more distinction, being the first indication that powerful politicians had taken up the issue of the radical element in

American life and, further, were prepared to use it regardless of the damage.[47]

In linking slavery with Southern opposition to internal improvements, Seward ignored the fact that the South, since colonial times, before slavery had become a national issue, had opposed spending government money to benefit particular interests. Seward, who had not previously pressed the attack on slavery, now realized how useful the issue was. Any Southern position could be blamed on slavery. John Quincy Adams had shown that inclination.

Soon every issue that seemed to compromise the economic interests of the North was attributed to the malign intentions of the "slaveocracy." The Whigs had discovered the issue that would trump the power that Democrats had wielded since the election of Jefferson to the presidency in 1800. Slavery was the wedge that would split Northern from Southern Democrats, the tool that could loosen the Democratic party's hold on power.

Lincoln saw the matter similarly. The night after his Cambridge appearance, he and Seward shared a hotel room, talking through the night about the slavery issue. According to Seward's son, Frederick, Lincoln told the father, "I have been thinking about what you said in your speech. I reckon you are right. We have got to deal with the slavery question and got to give more attention to it hereafter than we have been doing."[48]

There were precedents. In 1815 angry Northern Federalists at the Hartford Convention had begun complaining about the

---

[47] John M. Taylor, *William Henry Seward: Lincoln's Right Hand*, Harper Collins, 1991, p. 74; William C. Harris, *Lincoln's Rise to the Presidency*, University Press of Kansas, 2007, p. 51.

[48] Taylor, p. 51.

constitutional provision that added "three fifths of all other Persons" — slaves, that is — to the number of "free Persons" who were to be counted for the apportioning of representatives. The fight, in 1820-21, over admitting Missouri as a slave state was further kindling for the fire. Every issue, it seemed, could be used to stigmatize the South. Whatever the Southern position, it could be attacked as coming from the wicked "slaveholders," the "slaveocracy," the "Slave Power."

The South asked that the issue remain undisturbed by politicians, left to die of natural, as distinguished from political, causes. But the Democratic Party was strong, both in the North and the South. The Whigs needed an issue to divide the Democrats. Slavery was obviously the one. Lincoln's interest was not to solve the question but, rather, to use it as political leverage. And he used it more skillfully than Seward, who though milder than Lincoln, was perceived as too extreme on the slavery issue. It cost him the nomination in 1860. Lincoln was the more clever of the two Whig leaders.

Following his foray to Massachusetts, Lincoln traveled by train to Albany, where he visited Thurlow Weed, Whig boss of New York. The two of them visited Millard Fillmore, Whig candidate for vice-president. Then Lincoln went by way of the Erie Canal to Buffalo, thence to Lake Erie and overland to Chicago and Springfield. He arrived home in October to campaign for the Whig ticket. He traveled the state, campaigning for the Whigs. To his dismay, Illinois voted for Cass in November. The Whig ticket of Taylor and Fillmore was elected, but the local Whig was defeated in his run for Lincoln's seat by a Democrat and Mexican War veteran.

Lincoln's reputation had tainted his party even in Illinois's most Whiggish district. Lincoln had tried hard to turn the issue of the Mexican War to his advantage. It cost him and his party the election. The bitter lesson taught him by his speeches against the Mexican War would be the basis of his strategy in 1861 at Fort Sumter, facing a government determined to break with the United States.

In December Lincoln went back to Washington for his last congressional session. The Capitol rang with debates on the slavery issue. In January 1849, he planned to introduce a bill to abolish slavery in the District of Columbia. He said he had the backing of 15 of the town's leading citizens. Asked to name them, he failed to do so. John C. Calhoun, with less than a year to live, came forth in opposition. The "Southern Address," crafted by Calhoun and signed by 40 percent of the members of Congress from the slaveholding states, put the matter forthrightly. To destroy the existing relationship between the free and the servile races in the South, Calhoun insisted, would lead to consequences unparalleled in history. The result of emancipation, he said, "would be the prostration of the whole race" because the liberated Negroes would gain the right to vote and hold political office, would form political alliances with Northerners, and would control the patronage in the Southern states, thus rendering the South the "permanent abode of disorder, anarchy, poverty, misery, and wretchedness."[49] The slavery issue drove all other business away from consideration.

Congress adjourned, deadlocked, on Sunday, March 4, 1849. Lincoln remained in Washington for two months, exerting every resource he had in seeking a political appointment. Lincoln's party had won the election and had offices to dispense to its

---

[49] John C. Calhoun, "The Address of Southern Delegates in Congress, to Their Constituents," in *The Papers of John C. Calhoun*, Vol. XVI, Clyde N. Wilson ed., University of South Carolina, Press, 2001, p. 240.

partisans, but he could not get one. He sought appointment as Commissioner of the General Land Office, a powerful and potentially profitable position, although one without much political advancement opportunity. He made overtures to his friends, wrote letters to agents, and had a personal interview with President Taylor, giving him 11 reasons why he ought to have the job. But a man who had done less hack work than Lincoln was given the appointment. He was considered for governor of the Oregon Territory but failed to gain the position. The only offer he got was secretary of the Oregon Territory, an inconsequential post with a non-political future. Lincoln declined it. His hard work for a political appointment had alienated a faction of his party back home, where in any case the Democrat Cass had beaten the Whig Taylor. The Illinois Whigs were weak anyway. They could do nothing for him. The national Whig party had rewarded his extraordinary party work with an offer that was an insult. Lincoln was devastated. He was nearly 40 years old. For his entire adult life he had devoted himself assiduously to political advancement, had pursued with skill and energy a political career, and had ended with nothing. He was defeated. There was no other choice but to go home and go back to his trade, the practice of law. It was his last choice. Lincoln had lost; Clay had lost. Clay cried. Lincoln brooded.

Perfecting the Style

Lincoln had been to Washington. He had sat in the seats of the mighty. Now he was home, his seat in a back room of his office. He sat there long hours, slouched down, feet stretched on another chair, thinking and brooding. Herndon did most of the work for a while. Politics, political power was what Lincoln wanted, not the routine of a law practice in a country town. Lincoln "dripped melancholy," his friends said. He wrote a letter to Taylor's Secretary of State, John M. Clayton, declaring that Taylor's non-political approach to filling political offices was a great error and was hurting the party. Lincoln said the administration should reward loyal Whigs. Lincoln sat and thought. What had he done wrong?

He reached some conclusions. He had lost out because he had been against the Mexican War. Any proposition can be stated positively or negatively. If you are for something, you are against its opposite. A proposition can be stated attractively or repellently. Distant events are viewed simply. To succeed in politics, you must represent yourself as for a good thing. Your opponent, by definition, opposes this good thing. When one side can be pictured as being against a good cause, that side is immediately on the defensive. Therefore, the correct strategy is to find an issue, or create one, that positions you on the side of the angels, leaving your opponent to show how and why he is not serving the dark side.

Having learned this principle, Lincoln never forgot it. His stand on the Mexican War had cost him his job. It was a bitter lesson he would never forget. For the rest of his career he assiduously couched every issue. The South, which for valid economic and political reasons opposed Whig business subsidy policy, could be stigmatized as "against freedom." Every difference between the sections could be attributed to slavery. By 1861 Lincoln had honed that principle to razor sharpness. At Fort Sumter he craftily produced and directed the drama, even writing the text: The South had fired on Old Glory!

Lincoln talked to Herndon about his desire to do great things. He told Joshua Speed that he wanted glory. The great things, the glory was not yet to be. Three thousand four hundred Democrats, in 1849, were turned out of political jobs and replaced with 3,400 Whigs. But Lincoln was not among them. He lost his job and could not gain another one. Lincoln was never satisfied by his victories, but he was massively crushed by defeat. Herndon said that he despaired of ever rising again in the political world. "He was very sad and terribly gloomy."

Stephen Douglas, younger than Lincoln, after a brilliant career in the House of Representatives was now shining in the Senate. His success rankled Lincoln, who grudgingly and gradually returned to his law practice. To a Lincoln biographer anxious after the fact to make of Lincoln an eminent lawyer, Herndon said, "How are you going to make a great lawyer out of Lincoln? His soul was afire with its own ambition and that was not law." He thought constantly of politics. "His ambition was a little engine that knew no rest," said Herndon. Local politics had no charm for him. His ambition was to higher power. Meanwhile he practiced law.

It was a successful practice. Lincoln was a competent lawyer, though not a great one. He was good in argument — words came easily to him — but deficient in knowledge. That was the opinion of his fellows. Books have been written showing him as a legal Sir Galahad, defending the weak against the mighty, the innocent wrongly charged. That is stuff and nonsense. He took the side that paid him, like most other lawyers. For six months in the year he rode the court circuit, the only lawyer of his standing who continued to travel about. He enjoyed the social nature of the circuit, and it was the best way to make ready for the next political opportunity. He got to know all the local leaders in Illinois, and they got to like him. He was witty, smooth, attractive, a leader in any gathering. He courted popularity and was careful what he said. He liked the circuit. It gave him entertainment, variety, audience, and a political foundation for his next venture. And he made money. He and Herndon had a good practice.

After returning from Congress he began to travel more widely over the state, probably to promote his political position by expanding his political connections. He spent more time in public places than any other lawyer in Illinois. He read no law and little general literature but studied politics more than any man, according to the other lawyers. Lincoln entertained groups of ordinary people, but he never unbent to equality with them or anybody else. While an entertaining speaker and teller of tales, he seems to have kept his own counsel. Law did not interfere with politics. His pen, voice, and energy never ceased working for the party. He advised job appointments on the basis of party service, not merit. The Springfield postmaster opposed him politically. Lincoln worked to get him out.

In July 1849, his father-in-law, Robert Todd — bank president, cotton mill owner, one of the most prominent men in Kentucky — died, leaving a comfortable estate. Lincoln found no hindrance to leaving his work and travelling to Lexington, on the occasion of his father-in-law's death. On the occasion of his own father's decline, sickness, and death, at a shorter distance, Lincoln was too busy to leave his law practice.

He found a valuable friend in Judge David Davis, who presided over the Eighth Illinois Circuit Court, where Lincoln practiced. They spent much time together on the circuit, and it was Davis who directed the maneuvers that gained his friend the Republican presidential nomination in 1860. Lincoln later appointed him to the United States Supreme Court. His practice and business interests carried him to other areas, once to Cincinnati to represent a company accused of infringing on McCormick Reaper patents. A colleague in the case was the eminent lawyer, Edwin McMasters Stanton, from Pennsylvania, a man of doubtful character whom, seven years later, Lincoln would make Secretary of War.

In 1850, William Wallace Lincoln, the family's third son was born.

Lincoln successfully defended the Illinois Central Railroad from the attempt of a county to tax it. The railroad gave out of money and couldn't pay his $5,000 fee. Lincoln sued and got it. He used the money in his political comeback. He won friends in Chicago and in Illinois by being on the winning side in a dispute between the river interests of St. Louis and the railroad interests of Chicago. He got from this case notice, prestige, money, and connection with the powerful railroads, the country's fastest growing business. Money was going into railroads; where money goes, the power is sure to follow. And the power seekers.

He rose to high position in the legal profession, but law was merely a path to something higher. It was politics Lincoln loved and power he sought. Though he was a successful and important lawyer, he gave his highest and never-flagging attention to politics. Some people considered Lincoln a cunning, designing lawyer and politician, an ambitious man who coldly figured all his moves in advance. His lawyer friend Asa Whitney said that Lincoln picked his companions by what they could do for him. On the circuit he played billiards for hours with the same unattractive lawyer for the reason that he was as bad a player as Lincoln. Whitney said Lincoln never did anything without a reason except shoot pool.

Legend holds that Lincoln won his law cases through almost superhuman ability. No scrap of evidence supports such a claim. The fact is, he won some cases and lost others. Legend puts him on the right side of every case. The record shows that he sided with the clients who paid him — fighting them in the event they were slow to pay.

Illinois was filling fast with new settlers. It was plain to see that the people from Kentucky, Tennessee, Virginia, and the Carolinas who had once controlled Illinois were to be outnumbered and outvoted by the newcomers from the Northern states. Irish, German and English immigrants were coming to Illinois directly from Europe. Lincoln bought a German language newspaper to better get at this group. He studied the German language to learn a few phrases to throw at the new settlers.

His letters in pursuit of political office never slacked off, and often ended with, "Let all be so quiet that the adversary shall never be notified." Such is not the practice of a candid or sincere man; it is the motto of a politician.

On the national scene, sectional conflict was resuming. In Congress, representation of Northern economic interests was fast increasing and reducing the proportion of Southern representation. The South, which had controlled 46 percent of seats in the House of Representatives in 1789, held only 38 percent in 1850. There was a corresponding drop in the region's Electoral College strength. Only in the Senate did the South maintain equality with the North. The Union at that point comprised 15 free and 15 slave states. Meanwhile the Northern newcomers and the commercial and manufacturing interests wanted government money spent to make them some money. The South had always opposed internal improvements, and the hostility to the South, once held only by the New Englanders and some others in the lower Northeast, was now beginning to be manifest in the Northwestern states. These people wanted to make money, and they wanted government money to help them do it. The South was losing power as steadily as the North was gaining it.

California's prospective admission to the Union — as a free state — was the catalyst for nearly explosive examination of the country's widening divisions. The South saw its claim to parity with the North starting to slip away irretrievably. Jefferson Davis of Mississippi became anxious that as the balance of power shifted in favour of the North, the minority — Southerners — faced the loss of their accustomed protections. From Davis's state arose the call for a Southern rights convention to meet in Nashville and consider secession from the Union. Just at this point, the so-called Compromise of 1850 deflected the crisis, but it was notable how many of the agreement's provisions contravened Southern interests. The Compromise did re-state the federal law of 1793 requiring the return of fugitive slaves. This was merely a sop to Southern feelings, for only 200 slaves were ever in that category. But the Northern abolitionists took the Fugitive Slave Law and used it for a wild propaganda attack, and it did inflame Northern hostility toward the South. California duly came in as a free state. Also in the compromise was abolition of the slave trade in the District of Columbia. The compromise did not speak to the subject of slavery extension, but the general assumption was that the Missouri Compromise still stood, with slavery allowed below Latitude 36 31', prohibited above it.

In February 1850, Edward Baker ("Eddie") Lincoln died, a month short of his fourth birthday: possibly of a hereditary thyroid cancer. The funeral was conducted in the Presbyterian Church. The Lincolns became friendly with the minister and rented a pew in the Church. Mrs. Lincoln subsequently left the Episcopal Church and joined the Presbyterian Church. Lincoln, asked whether he would join also, said he "couldn't quite see it."

He never could "quite see" religion. Except as a public gathering place the church did not interest him, nor, except as a subject to liven his speeches, did religion much interest him. He used the Bible as a model for literary style and the Scriptures to illustrate his points, sometimes changing their original context to achieve his ends. A secular man, he embraced the deistical, anti-Christian outlook fashionable with Ralph Waldo Emerson and the New England intellectuals. At the same time he was superstitious to a foolish extent.

Herndon had a library of works popular with the intellectuals of the period, secular and humanistic. Of that spring he drank deeply. Their doctrine was the 19th century humanism that ultimately precipitated the American Civil War, together with Marxism and most of the troubles of the 20th Century. The Sophists were not new, just back in fashion. The philosophy is old — a man-centered heresy, dividing Christianity and Christ, presenting ways to attain salvation without the Savior, trying to make God man, and man God. Lincoln did not read deeply in them, but he did scan and swallow them. Both Herndon and James H. Matheny, best men at his wedding, considered Lincoln to be an "infidel." Jesse W. Fell said that Lincoln held the views of Theodore Parker and William Ellery Channing, spokesmen of the leftist humanist movement that spawned the violence of the slavery issue.

This is highly significant. Fell gave Lincoln a collection of Channing's sermons because Lincoln was so interested in Channing. On page 34 was a sentence "Ye have loved me, and have believed that I came forth from God." In Lincoln's volume, found on his bookshelf at home, the words "from God" are crossed out and replaced with the words in Lincoln's handwriting, "from nature." In Fell's sympathetic judgment Lincoln "did not believe in what are regarded as the orthodox or evangelical views" of Christianity. Rather, he believed in "the Fatherhood of God and the Brotherhood of Man."[50]

True, Lincoln knew the Bible, having been raised on it by two good mothers and a God-fearing father who believed in and lived by it. Lincoln knew the Bible for other reasons when he became grown. His interest in it was, as religious source, slight; as literature and philosophy, casual; concerning style, profound; as a tool — a model useful in communicating and necessary to a political career, zealous.

He not only knew his Bible, he used it: as illustration in talking to jurors, in political speeches, in politics, and in letters. The Bible was idiom. Many less-close acquaintances considered him a solemn, earnest, religious man. Selected to deliver the eulogy for President Zachary Taylor in Chicago, Lincoln spoke solemnly, and in a religious mode. He was the best speaker in the Whig Party. He spent weeks on his speeches, all of which were based on his 1838 Lyceum speech. The King James Bible's spare style directed him.

When Lincoln learned in 1851 that his father was dying, he wrote his step-mother's son, John D. Johnston, a letter interesting to ponder, showing his awareness of his own importance and his

---

[50] Wilson and Davis, p. 579.

lack of interest in his dying father. He had two excuses, rather than just one, for not coming to visit Thomas Lincoln. He demonstrated his rare ability to communicate, whatever the occasion and his facility with the Bible, the tool he used, but did not believe.

"I feel sure," he wrote, "you have not failed to use my name, if necessary to procure a doctor, or anything else for father in his sickness. My business is such that I could hardly leave home now, if it was not as it is, that my own wife is sick-a-bed. (It is a case of baby-sickness, and I suppose is not dangerous.) I sincerely hope father may recover his health, but at all events, tell him to remember to call upon and confide in our great and good merciful Maker, who will not turn away from him in any extremity. He notes the fall of a sparrow, and numbers the hairs of our heads, and he will not forget the dying man who puts his trust in Him. Say to him that if we could meet now it is doubtful whether it would not be more painful than pleasant, but that if it be his lot to go now, he will soon have a joyous meeting with many loved ones gone before, and where the rest of us, through the help of God, hope ere long to join them."[51]

What did he mean by "a meeting more painful than pleasant?" This could only refer to an estrangement between father and son caused by the son's ambition exceeding filial duty, an honest admission that he had, in life shown no interest in his father or mother.

---

[51] Lincoln, *Speeches and Writings*, Vol. 1, pp. 255-256.

Storm Watch

THERE SEEMED TO BE, AMONG THOSE who wielded influence in the North, no national concern except those dividing the nation. The Negro was to be used as an issue for white men to gain power. A rising crescendo of drumbeats was being heard, magnifying every issue concerning Northern and Southern economic interests and political power. In the attempt to win for its side, the North had learned — to a large degree from the wily and bitter John Quincy Adams — that the South's position on every subject could be attributed to slavery and the North's to superior morality. When politics strikes morality, a fire is ignited. More and more politicians from the North were explaining every issue by calling the South a nation of evil. Automatic stigma was to be the fate of the Southerner henceforward.

In 1831 the abolition movement began to grow. Southerners became surprised, alarmed, and indignant at the rising hostility directed towards them. Few slaves ran away. Those who did, tended to carry individual grievances — by no means an indication of maltreatment.

The "Underground Railway" — the informal network conveying runaway slaves in great secrecy to safety in the North — was much publicised but amounted to little in fact. Southerners stated publicly that the Fugitive Slave Law was only a sop to the South's pride, a matter of no real substance, passed in order to tell the South that the law would be followed. It was really more of a statement to recognize the right of slaveowners to reclaim their runaway slaves than a law to enforce that right. The Compromise favoured the Northern political faction. By 1850 symbolic rights, theory, and abstract principles often assumed greater importance in the thinking of individuals than did the concrete problems of real life. Thus it is through the ages.

Quickly discovering that the Compromise of 1850 was a useful propaganda weapon, abolitionists held meetings to inflame opinion and concocted ways to discredit the compromise itself. Congress members in the antislavery camp — men such as Joshua Giddings and Benjamin F. Wade of Ohio and Charles Sumner of Massachusetts — raised a hue and cry. Various states enacted laws declaring the Fugitive Slave law — a constitutional federal enactment — null and void in their territory. Lincoln never opposed that exercise of states' rights. Abolitionists violated federal law deliberately. (Later, in 1854, the Kansas-Nebraska Bill was an issue similarly used by the abolitionists to create a furor.) The North was clearly willful and constitutionally unjustified in putting aside a duly enacted law of Congress in order to serve its own political ends. Northerners piled upon their Southern countrymen every term of abuse that came to mind — "criminals," "pirates," "aristocrats," "lazy," and so on and so on. If rarely enforced, the Fugitive Slave law did its work for the abolitionists, feeding their fervor, confirming their anti-South viewpoint.

The South knew what was afoot. Northern-born Congressman John A. Quitman of Mississippi said that the Fugitive Slave article of the Compromise of 1850 was no more than a blind to hide the vast sacrifices demanded of the South. Congressman W.O. Goode of Virginia said, "The re-enactment in 1850 of the Fugitive Slave law of 1793 only served to afford the North an opportunity to re-enact the insulting violations of the rights of the South by a disregard of all social, moral, religious, legal, and constitutional obligations.[52] "The law was no more than an opportunity for the abolitionist to raise a false issue. In that sense it was a powerful success."

Zachary Taylor was a Southern slaveholder, his position as president being somewhat similar to that of Andrew Jackson in that he was advised by the financial interests of the North and that his closest advisor was the leading politician of New York. Jackson had Van Buren, and Taylor had William Seward. A decade later Seward, who had advised one of the nation's most powerful slaveholders, would become advisor to the nation's greatest abolitionist, making war against Taylor's son Richard and son-in-law Jefferson Davis, who risked all defending their country against the aggression of Seward's chief. What better proof that the motive force in politics and war is desire for power, not principles?

Webster, Clay, and Calhoun died. New men appeared — the most brilliant of whom was Stephen A. Douglas of Illinois. Commercial and industrial interests in the North were manufacturing an avalanche of demands for government money. The Northern people were steadily uniting in their desire for government money as they became, especially in the East, less agricultural. In the Northwest the young economy, too, wanted government help. These tensions had split the Democratic party into two factions. National issues fueled the rivalry for power. Senators Sumner of Massachusetts and Salmon P. Chase of Ohio were among the founders of the so-called Free Soil party, which offered Van Buren for the presidency in 1848, against Cass and Taylor. Party members — future Republicans all — blamed

---

[52] Larry Gara, *The Liberty Line: The Legend of the Underground Railroad*, University Press of Kentucky, 1961, p. 129.

national ills on a slaveowners' conspiracy. Their stance gave them a following, but Congress's dominant figure after the deaths or retirements of Calhoun, Clay, and Webster was Douglas of Illinois — the Little Giant, a man of massive head and shoulders, with intellect to match; well-suited to leadership by temperament as by intellect.

The Whigs narrowly won with Zachary Taylor in 1848, but Taylor was non-political — a slaveowner with a national outlook, doubtful that slavery was to be regarded as a serious issue. Victory did not bring power to the party. The upright Taylor died July 9, 1850, and was succeeded by his vice-president, the upright Millard Fillmore of New York, a member of the Whig party's Clay faction. Neither man sought to strengthen the Whig party. In 1852 the Whigs tried to win by nominating another Mexican war hero, General Winfield Scott. But Franklin Pierce a New Hampshire Democrat who had served in the war under Scott, routed his old commander at the polls. His victory killed the party to which Lincoln had given so much devotion, and in which he had reposed such large hopes.

Lincoln would have to look elsewhere for ingresses to power. He stayed busy politicking, working on speech-making, reading a book on logic to make use of its terms in his speeches. He was always ready to address the public. In one speech to the Scott Club in Springfield, answering a speech Douglas made in Richmond, Illinois, Lincoln showed so nakedly his envy of Douglas that his friends were embarrassed for him.

The election of Pierce, a Northerner who represented all regions, was on the surface a healing balm. In fact, his victory covered over a festering cancer. The Northern commercial interests had a growing political faction that would, in 1860 bring them victory. Its roots went back to 1800 when the Adamses were, in effect, dethroned by Thomas Jefferson and his followers. That faction wanted revenge, and a return to power. Jackson and John Tyler had de-railed the prospects of the capitalist clan. The victory of the conservative Polk killed Van Buren's chances but not his ambition.

Denied the presidency in 1848 — Van Buren's 291,000 votes as a Free Soiler may have thrown the election to Taylor — the former vice president's faction was considerable in size and influence. Its members bided their time. Pierce's constituency, and that of James Buchanan, Secretary of State under Polk, spread across the nation but still excluded the monied factions. Ahead lay the downfall of the Democrats due to factional fighting between the two most powerful of their ilk — Buchanan of Pennsylvania and the redoubtable Stephen A. Douglas, whose destiny was bound up with Lincoln's own.

The election of Pierce marked a period of even-handed treatment of both sections, North and South. This balance had existed under Zachary Taylor, and would continue throughout the 1850s, under the administrations of Fillmore and Buchanan. The Democratic party did have a Northern wing, reflecting and serving the rising commercial and industrial groups, adding the reason of economic self-interest to the simple power rivalry that had made the old New England Federalists and Whigs oppose the South. The Democratic party was now the only national party (with the exception of the small American, or "Know Nothing," party, which opposed immigration). The Republican party and the Free-Soil party were bitterly sectional. The Democrats were bound together by common interests. Their leaders wanted victory and as many votes as necessary and possible. They wanted to make both sections happy. They were thus a unifying force, tending to lessen sectional division. For the non-Democrats, disharmony was necessary to dislodging their rivals from the dominance they had enjoyed since 1800.

First the Federalists, and now the Whigs, were dead. It was impossible for their remnants to get votes in the South. They had to divide in order to conquer. They had to alienate the Northern Democrats from the South. And thus, although the administration of Pierce sought to heal wounds and apply balm, the powerless Whig remnant that would soon transform itself into the Republican party looked around like Iago, seeking to destroy Othello.

Unaware what fate awaited them, the Democrats were basking in complacency. A Democrat held the Presidency. In the Senate, Douglas of Illinois was as illustrious as Lincoln was forgotten. And Lincoln knew it. He and Herndon discussed it daily.

Rejected power-seekers in the North were now without a machinery for power. There were too many of them for this power vacuum to remain empty or quiet. And they were not quiet.

In the meantime, Douglas had taken the prize that Lincoln wanted. As the most articulate member of the Senate from the Midwest, Douglas was for western expansion. Movement was blocked by the need to give political organisation to the territories west of the Missouri river called Nebraska. Some form of local rule had to be established; local government in the form of a territory had to be created; statehood would follow. It was through these lands that Douglas, representing the interests of Illinois, hoped to run the transcontinental railroad that would join the East to California. Local politics in Iowa called for splitting the territory into a northern half (Nebraska) and a southern half (Kansas).

Kansas lay due west of Missouri, and Missouri politics controlled Kansas. In Missouri the fight for political control was between the rival Democratic senators David Rice Atchison and Thomas Hart Benton. By assuming that the Missouri

Compromise of 1820 had been repealed by the Compromise of 1850 Douglas could help Atchison and get votes for the northern railway route instead of the more southern route favoured by Jefferson Davis, Secretary of War. Douglas, motivated by no more than his own desire (and duty, as chairman of the Committee on Territories) to make some accommodation that would get the territorial status established, and allow the railway construction to be authorised, wrote a bill to this end. It was his job to do so. He introduced to his committee a bill allowing settlers in the new territories to vote for the introduction of slavery should they desire it. This option, called "popular sovereignty," applied only to the southern half of the territory, to Kansas; but the great agitation it caused came while the name Nebraska was still applied to the whole area west of the Missouri River.

Douglas introduced on January 23, 1854, his bill for organising the territories of Kansas and Nebraska and permitting the people of those territories to allow or not allow slavery. In effect the bill repealed the Missouri Compromise. A day later, Senators Sumner and Chase issued their manifesto, "The Appeal of the Independent Democrats in Congress to the People of the United States," attacking Douglas's bill as part of a never-ending conspiracy of the slave states to extend slavery. It was a call to arms. This innocent bill gave the nudge to the war engine. The anti-Democrat faction used it as a much-needed means of rallying public support.

The power vacuum created by the decline of the Federalist-Whig partisans had made a market for any politician who could find an issue to rally opposition to the dominant Democrats. The rejected Whigs and the angry "Free Soilers" of 1848 rallied at once to the "Anti-Nebraska Cause." Many Northern Democrats defied President Pierce and joined them. Chase and Sumner had laboured for years alone to create an opposition party. Now they had their adherents. They had found an issue. In fact, they had not "found" the issue. They had created it. The whole Kansas-Nebraska affair was a fraud, a fire ignited to advance the careers of a faction.

Senator Seward, the most important survivor of the derelict Whig party, joined the clamour. That was a bad sign. Seward was astute and influential. Douglas as usual, took the hornets' attack manfully. Nobody could have foreseen the fury of the storm.

The bill passed only because of Democratic party discipline. It would have been better for Douglas, for the country, and for the well-being of 700,000 Americans who lost their lives in the war it caused if the bill had failed. There is no question that this bill became a vehicle to advance the ambitions of politicians and brought on a war. If Douglas and Buchanan had not fallen out, war would have not occurred. It should be noted that this legislation had not been asked for by the South. The Southern position was that territories could not decide the issue of slavery. Only when they became states could they do so.

The bill made Lincoln's career and was the first of a series of fortuitous accidents that saved the Republicans and carried Lincoln to the presidency. The schism in the Democratic party and the decay of the Whig party — that is, the power vacuum — caused two new parties to appear. The first was the American party, the "Know Nothings." Asked to define their platform (which included opposition to public office for Catholics and aliens and literacy tests for voting), members were instructed to say, "I know nothing." They were to profess ignorance, supposedly, in order to attract interest. This party was a Northern reaction to the flood of German and Irish immigrants that began pouring into the country in the late 1840s.

The party was at first popular. Many Old Whigs joined it. It was a seed-bed for anti-Nebraska Democrats and Whigs to coalesce into the Republican Party.

CAUTIOUSLY REPUBLICAN

THE REPUBLICAN PARTY WAS BORN in 1854 from the campaign against Douglas. For power, not for principle. Douglas had alienated the Buchanan Democrats, the schism being due to power not principle. The Whig Party had died. Two groups of politicians were without power. The Northern people wanted the Negroes kept South. They wanted to migrate to territories devoid of black people, free or slave. Thus, available politicians, (unemployed but seeking power) found the issue that would further their ruling objective. Douglas's bill had afforded that opportunity at precisely the right moment for these particular politicians. Searching for a flattering name, they seized on "Republican," a name embedded in the name of Thomas Jefferson's Democratic-Republican party. The Democrats had always claimed to be the spiritual heirs of Jefferson. The new party now challenged that claim. The name "Republican" was non-committal as to content and philosophical direction and made membership in the new party more palatable for seceding Democrats.

From its beginning the Republican party was fixed on narrow sectional interests: resistance to the so-called "Slave Power." There was not in fact such a thing as "the slave power," but the epithet, the slogan, served its purpose, creating in the mind of the ignorant the notion that an organized evil faction planned to take over control of America. The political leaders from the decomposing Whig Party had sullenly watched the Democratic Party politicians enjoy power almost undisturbed since the defeat of John Adams and the Federalists in 1800. Except for the incomplete victory of John Quincy Adams in 1824 they had been excluded from power. The few Whigs who had won the presidency had done little or nothing to strengthen the party of non-Democrats.

Van Buren's Democratic faction had formed a nucleus after his defeat for the nomination by Polk. This group and others who resented Douglas's dominance in the Democratic Party had found a way to injure their successful antagonists: take up the abolition issue and make it political; call the Democrats an evil "slave power." Take up, in short, an, issue that was bound to alarm the South, which had most of its capital tied up in slaves. Concerted Northern hostility to the South had been predicted in 1787 by George Mason and in 1816 by John Randolph of Roanoke. Let the Abolitionists supply the noise; the politicians and their backers would supply the money.

They called Douglas the tool of the slave-power conspiracy, a calumny that they themselves could hardly have believed, and that in any case was proven wrong in 1860 when the slave states refused to vote for Douglas, or even assist in his nomination to the presidency. The anti-Douglas group vowed to punish all Douglas supporters as betrayers of the North; never mind that Douglas was criticized in the South as not strong enough in support of the Democratic position.

Here we see the weakness, yet the essence, of the democratic form of government; i.e., power lodged in the mass of people. The system produces demagogues seeking power who will say anything and do anything to get it. Opponents wanted the power Douglas held, and would shrink from no demagogy to get it. "Kansas-Nebraska" was an artificial issue, a hypocritical falsehood, created solely for political gain.

As chairman of the Committee on Territories, Douglas said that the territory west of Illinois, meaning Nebraska and Kansas, needed to be put into some legal form so that settlement, government, law, railroad construction, and trade could be commenced in an orderly fashion. Out of this desire came his "popular sovereignty" bill: the people living in the territories could vote to make slavery legal or illegal. The federal government, ruled out of the slavery issue by the Constitution of the United States, would not take part in the decision. Douglas addressed the problem and suggested a practical solution. He said economics and geography dictated there would never be slavery in either state. There were two slaves in Kansas, none in Nebraska.

But Douglas, by the definition of his political opponents, was a scoundrel. Overnight the issue burst into flames. The train ride that Douglas made back to Illinois is famous for the bonfires of aroused citizens burning him in effigy. "They lighted his way home." Douglas manfully spoke up to this crowd in Chicago and at the Springfield State Fair. He said accurately that the politicians had taken the territorial bill to ridiculous extremes in opposing popular sovereignty. Douglas' viewpoint was practical, down-to-earth: Let the people decide. Lincoln, by contrast, in addressing the same issue, affected a vague but incendiary manner.

Lincoln's speeches had two forms. The original style was aggressive, full of contemptuous ridicule. He was now moving into a new style he had been perfecting, imitating the calm, measured delivery of Calhoun, without Calhoun's facts — abstract, religious; affecting a moral superiority but always carefully avoiding any practical detail that could pin him down. First, he condemned the ownership of slaves. Then he quickly added, "Let it not be said I am contending for the establishment of political and social equality between the whites and the blacks. I have already said the contrary."

He extracted a single phrase from the Declaration of Independence and ignored the Constitution. "All men are created equal," he kept saying. He called one side (his own) the side of God; the other side, as he portrayed it — that of Mammon — wished that slavery might be extended to the white race. The immigrants could not be faulted for believing they, too, would be enslaved. They and the older citizens opposed allowing black people to move into Illinois who would take their jobs. Illinois — Lincoln's own state — passed a law to exclude Negroes from the territory, free or slave. He stirred their emotions; he was a performer.

Lincoln had shown his greatest asset — an ability to avoid detail but raise a preacher's voice in a metaphysical moral tone which was safely vague and left him safely uncommitted. He said that slavery was wrong, and that the Southerners were guilty of destroying the Declaration of Independence. (Never mind that the document was written by a slaveholder!) Any proposition can be stated positively or negatively. Choose an issue and frame it positively so that the "enemy" is portrayed as opposing some great good.

Lincoln, as we have seen again and again, was always in search of an issue. Now he had one. He put a moral onus on Douglas for taking a practical and honest view of slavery. Slavery did exist, and it was not fair to those already involved in it, as owners or supporters, to start calling them criminals. Douglas was honest. Lincoln was on safe grounds because he never became specific. What he did was calculated, dishonest, a subterfuge. It gave the average unthinking citizen a moral cause, never mind its truth, its consequences. The speech was pretty, but meaningless. He was a master of words, but the conclusion sanctioned violence. The idea he worked so hard in giving to the fresh immigrants from Germany and Ireland, who were a substantial bloc of voters, is that they would next be enslaved. Douglas said that Lincoln had been more troublesome than all the opposition speeches he had heard in the Senate.

The anti-Douglas forces carried the state legislature, which was to elect a U.S. Senator. Would they elect Lincoln? He hinted, worked, "almost cried," his friend William Jayne said. He was on the alert now. He wanted to be the choice of the legislature. He wrote letters. But the Republicans were reluctant to give the Senate seat to a man who was not yet a Republican. Lincoln missed becoming senator by three votes. Lyman Trumbull, a Democrat who had had the courage to declare himself and join the anti-Nebraska faction, was selected. The Illinois voters wanted to migrate to Kansas and Nebraska. They did not want Negroes to go there, too. That was the sentiment the antislavery politicians were agitating.

Lincoln was beaten again and humbled again. His eager seeking of the job gave him an unseemly thirst that made him stay in the running too long. He did not withdraw soon enough to acquire any party merit, and his Whig partisans were angry enough to strain the alliance. It was the greatest blow so far to his political aspirations.

But this time Lincoln did not have to withdraw into a depressing retirement as he had after losing his congressional seat in 1846 and after the collapse of the Whigs in 1850. For the alliance created by the contest for Nebraska, the "anti-Nebraska" group was holding together and riding a popular issue. Lincoln still avoided an open commitment to the Republicans, but as the wave of popular indignation at the somewhat manufactured Nebraska affair began to quieten, events in Kansas came to the rescue. The influx of English, German, and Irish immigrants into Northern Illinois had changed the composition of the electorate. They feared the competition of Negro labour. They did not want the Negroes to come into their territory. What Douglas had written in the bill to form new territories had been done innocently, but the majority of voters in the Midwest wanted the Negroes excluded from settlement of the new territories.

The application of the doctrine of "popular sovereignty" in Kansas was not proving as easy as Douglas had thought it would. Pro-slavery and anti-slavery factions, including insurgents sent in and paid for the purpose, were turning Kansas into a battleground. Organized armed bands, subsidized by wealthy interests in the North, stirred the pot. Disputed elections, rival constitutions, and armed violence occurred. The new territory acquired the name "Bleeding Kansas." As long as Kansas bled, the new party had an issue that could stir the public. The anti-Douglas press and the Republican Party wanted discord. They wanted Kansas to bleed, and influential New England abolitionists provided the weapons to make it bleed.

Lincoln was one of the politicians who wanted Kansas to bleed. His career depended upon it. However, it seems obvious that ambition explains only part of his position. Evidence is plentiful that Lincoln, deny it as he did, was in fact an abolitionist, whatever might be his motives. He was a perfect expression of the abolitionist: an ambitious lawyer, with a good practice; a superficial intellectual who had rejected traditional religion and espoused all the contemporary liberal views; not orthodox in religion (he belonged to no church), rather a follower of the humanistic secular doctrine of the Unitarian clergyman William Ellery Channing and the anti-slavery theologian Theodore Parker, who would encourage and help finance John Brown's raid on Harper's Ferry. There is no question as to Lincoln's being a perfect reflection of the stylish intellectual view of his time. He scoffed at Jesus but never forgot the value of using His name.

Lincoln lacked wisdom enough to see through the thin Rousseau-Emerson world view, to oppose it with classical instruction. At the same time and perhaps for the same reason he was too "elevated" to subscribe to Christian faith. He was a man of action and himself wanted to "be as a god" — a deus ex machina, taking action, moving the world, and enjoying, correspondingly, the world's notice. This impulse comes from within man himself. It caused the French Revolution, Lincoln's Revolution, the Russian Revolution, and explains the approval such movements incite. Man wants to be God, to take action.

Even in 1854 Lincoln was accused of being an abolitionist; he always denied it. To admit it was political suicide. He struck terror in the hearts of the Southerners and proved their fears. They knew his true views. Events confirmed them. He never stopped saying "all men are created equal" and in the abstract using that as justification for steps he denied in particular. He was demagogic as an abolitionist. On the Kansas-Nebraska question, he castigated the opposite side as the party of violence repeatedly. He kept speaking of the slaves as living the life of "stripes and unequaled toil," when stripes were rare and a slave's toil was better requited than that of a Northern factory worker. He spoke of fugitive slaves as a great issue, when, all told, they numbered no more than 200. He falsely accused the South not only of slave trading but of slave breeding. He called the North moral and the South immoral, the kind of Manichean attack that Douglas eschewed. In Lincoln's eyes the South was controlled by slave owners, notwithstanding that only about one Southern white family in four owned any slaves whatever. Of this number, fully half owned no more than four slaves, and five-sevenths owned nine or fewer. It was some "slaveocracy," the South that Lincoln castigated so freely.

Clearly the larger planters — those with 40 or more slaves and at least 800 acres — wielded considerable influence but scarcely enough on their own to overawe the farmers of the region or the manufacturers, merchants, and members of the professional classes. Where was the slaveowners' irresistible power? Hostility to the mere principle of slavery extension made planters afraid to carry slaves worth $1500 into Kansas and Nebraska, where the Abolitionists clearly meant business. Lincoln himself subscribed $25 to a fund for buying weapons for the Northern faction in Kansas. Debating Douglas in 1858, he talked abolitionist language in ruling out prospects for survival of a nation half slave and half free.

Coming Out

THE 1856 PRESIDENTIAL ELECTION was pivotal in Lincoln's formation as a foe of the South. It now appeared that the Republicans, not the "Know Nothings," would inherit the Northern Whig voters. Illinois Republicans undertook to set their project on a forward-looking basis by means of an organisational meeting in Bloomington. On-fourth of the attendants were regularly appointed Republican delegates; the rest came on their own. All sorts and conditions of political leaders gathered there. Their common attribute was non-membership in the Democratic Party. They were Whigs, abolitionists, Free-Soilers, anti-Douglas Democrats, bolting Democrats, Know Nothings — a collection of politicians of any stripe outside the Democratic Party. It was a political gathering. Politicians are powerless without a party. A political party is a group of people clubbed together to seek power.

These men had one common need — a party. They had only one common issue — the need, as they saw it, to attack slavery. The people they represented did not want slaves (or free Negroes) admitted to their state or territory of interest. The Northern and foreign immigrants did not want Negroes where they lived. They wanted to keep them out, to make them stay in the South. The politicians were going to use that popular attitude as an avenue to power. The new Republican Party, launched officially in 1854, was really an anti-Democratic Party faction which had chosen the name for its association with the name of Thomas Jefferson's old "Democratic-Republican" Party. It was a pleasant title, but many politicians were still timid about actually joining a party called irresponsible by many others.

The cautious Lincoln had not joined. He understood, nevertheless, the direction of events, which was toward stiffness and resistance to Southern assertions of historic right under the constitutional form of government. He was having none of Stephen Douglas's popular sovereignty doctrine. At Springfield, October 4, 1854, he lashed Douglas' arguments for three hours, repeating the charges 12 days later at Peoria. His appeal that the Missouri Compromise be restored "for the sake of the Union" kept eccentric company with the feverish assertion that backers of the Kansas-Nebraska bill wished to establish a precedent for "the planting of slavery wherever in the wide world, local and unorganized opposition cannot prevent it." He nevertheless made a powerful impression on his audience. Ironically, the anti-slavery forces had voted against and condemned the Missouri Compromise, the repeal of which they were now treating as blasphemy.

Lincoln knew the dimensions of that impact. He waited; he listened. In 1856, he accepted election as a delegate to the convention in Bloomington, Illinois, where various opponents of slavery expansion, including Democrats and Know Nothings, meant to organise a state Republican party. The assemblage chose Lincoln as one of two presidential electors. Still, he yearned for the party to take real, and admiring, notice of him. Unscheduled to speak, operating mostly on the fringes of the meeting, he hungered to be called on for some remarks.

The convention was on the verge of adjournment when his moment came — a response to cries that were likely motivated, says Elwell De Crissey, by the desire to be sent home feasting on some Lincolnesque jokes and aphorisms. "[I]n a kindly way they were asking him to be their buffoon." He stood up with a show of reluctance. Then slowly, with deliberation, he began putting off the jester's motley. He became "fiery, emotional, reckless, violent, hot-blooded — everything which at other times he was not . . . a giant possessed," pouring forth a "stupendous flood of wrath and emotion." He spoke from scribbled notes. His listeners were captivated, thoughts of adjournment suddenly irrelevant. When he finished, an hour and a half after beginning, "a mob of frenzied men churned around him, congratulating him, praising him, pumping his hand."[53] Every issue needs rhetoric as propulsive power. Politics and rhetoric — those two words sum up the man.

The Bloomington speech delivered May 29, 1856, and known as Lincoln's "lost speech," has, for all its elusiveness to history, been cited numerous times as possibly the best of his life. It was likely, as well, the most inflammatory. According to legend, his listeners, a raft of newspaper reporters included, were so enraptured they neglected to take notes. No reports were published at the time, which suggests that Lincoln was not ready to broadcast his position to a wider audience.

What did he say? No version of the speech came to light for 40 years until *McClure's Magazine* published an account offered by a Lincoln admirer and biographer who had actually heard it delivered — Henry Clay Whitney. Whitney's rendition (complete with interpolations of audience reaction) was long taken as authentic, though modern scholars naturally hesitate to sanctify the text on one man's unsupported word. At any rate the Whitney

---

[53] Far the most thorough and meticulous account of the Bloomington address is to be found in Elwell De Crissey, *Lincoln's Lost Speech: The Pivot of His Career*, Hawthorn Books, 1967. De Crissey's grandfather was present on the occasion.

text burns with something like the righteous emotion that a speech of this kind would have kindled.[54]

Lincoln began — according to this chronicler — "Mr. Chairman and Gentlemen ... we can hardly be called delegates strictly, in as much as, properly speaking we represent nobody but ourselves .... We are in a trying time ... [u]nless popular opinion makes itself felt very strongly, and a change is made in our present course, blood will flow on account of Nebraska, and brother's hand will be raised against brother." He noted that the "delegates" had been collected from many different elements, yet they were all agreed that "Slavery must be kept out of Kansas." Douglas's Nebraska act (to allow territorial inhabitants to vote slavery in or out) was usurpation. The federal government (when controlled by Lincoln's faction) should outlaw it. If allowed to stand, it would result in opening all states to slavery.

"We are in a fair way to see this land of boasted freedom converted into a land of slavery in fact." He was providing the rhetoric necessary to justify a movement. It might be fake, it might be inflammatory; it might produce cruel results. It was by Lincoln's calculation necessary for the forming of a political party. Lincoln was blowing the war bugle, telling the audience members what they wanted to hear and needed to say to the nation — to stir up this issue — if they wanted their party to grow. The level of demagoguery rose: "I read once in a law book that a slave is a

---

[54] If Whitney faithfully reconstructed the speech years after its delivery, his must have been one of the most remarkable memories in human history. Care should be taken in appropriation of the exact wording reported by Whitney. On the other hand, his tone and tenor appear, from the general recollection of audience members, to be mostly if not entirely accurate.

human being who is legally not a person but a 'thing.' If the safeguards to liberty are broken down as is now attempted [in the Nebraska Act], when they have made 'things' of all the free Negroes, how long, think you, before they will begin to make 'things' of poor white men?"

Who could truly believe in such a possibility? Certainly Lincoln knew better. Certainly everybody in that hall knew better. These men were tough politicians, power-seekers and power makers. They had been out, they saw a way to get in. They had to have an issue; they couldn't let Kansas-Nebraska die. Lincoln was the Dr. Frankenstein who could raise the issue to life. He had the talent to do what needed to be done. That is what excited those men that day in Major's Hall.

Lincoln presented a history of the United States, saying that freedom and equality (mutually exclusive terms) sacred to the men of the American Revolution, had become words it was fashionable to sneer at. "Suppose Kansas comes in as a slave state, and all the 'border ruffians' have barbecues about it, and free state men come trailing back to the dishonored North, like whipped dogs with their tails between their legs, it is — ain't it? — evident that this is no more 'the land of the free.'" Lincoln, no moderate as he is depicted by history, was using the abolitionist term for the settlers in Kansas who came over from Missouri or the South.

Lincoln's assertion is unreasonable. If the settlers in the new territory had voted to allow slaves, would the others have left? Hardly. All the Nebraska bill did was to commission the settlers to decide the issue by a free vote — the approach called "squatter sovereignty" by Southerners who insisted that slavery could only be decide d by a state, not by the first settlers in a territory. No objective view of the matter made it seem likely that the economics of the new area could make the cotton-scented institution of slavery viable in the country's treeless and (in wintertime at least, frozen midlands). "[A]nd if we let [Kansas] go so," he added provocatively, "we won't dare to say 'home of the brave' out loud." (Whitney's account says the words excited "Sensation and confusion.")

Lincoln went on. Monstrous crimes were being committed in the name of slavery. The "slave power" (a favourite Abolitionist term to frighten the simple) was making steady advances by violence, craft, and intimidation. "Slavery is a violation of the eternal right. We have temporized with it from the necessities of our conditions; but it as sure as God reigns and school children read, THAT BLACK FOUL LIE CAN NEVER BE CONSECRATED INTO GOD'S HALLOWED TRUTH!" (Whitney records "immense applause lasting some time.") "The repeal of the sacred Missouri Compromise," said the increasingly passionate Lincoln, "has installed the weapon of violence: the bludgeon, the incendiary torch, the death-dealing rifle, the bristling cannon — the weapon of kingcraft, of the Inquisition, of ignorance, of barbarian, of oppression ...." He was sparing no lash-blows to the imagination. "... I will not say that we may not sooner or later meet force by force; but the time has not yet come, may never come. Do not mistake that the ballot is stronger than the bullet."

The climax was near. The Union, that "stout old ship," was undergoing "fearful strain." Americans were to "keep step to the music of the Union. Let us draw a cordon, so to speak, around the slave States, and the hateful institution, like a reptile poisoning itself, will perish by its own infamy .... We must highly resolve that Kansas shall be free .... We must make this a land of liberty in fact, as it is in name."

And if confronted by the South with threats of secession, what then? "WE WILL SAY TO THE SOUTHERN DISUNIONISTS, WE WON'T GO OUT OF THE UNION, AND YOU SHAN'T!!!" ("The audience," Whitney wrote, "rose to its feet en masse, applauded, stamped, waved handkerchiefs, threw hats in the air, and ran riot for several minutes. The arch-enchanter who wrought this transformation looked, meanwhile, like the personification of political justice.)

A few more fiery sentences, and the arch-enchanter — or arsonist, according to taste — was done, finishing his business with the entirely ironic appeal to "moderation and forbearance."

Historians generally agree: Truly lost or not, Lincoln's Bloomington speech vaulted him to something more than prominence among the foes of slavery; to eminence, actually. It served also to harden sentiment regarding disposition of the slavery question. If the question admitted of no compromise — "right" being on one side and not the other — "moderation and forbearance" were unlikely to show their faces as the country lurched toward division and war. Lincoln's line in the sand, so to call it, invited his hearers to stand together on one side, imagining all those on the other side to be malignant and hateful: worthy, perhaps, of eradication.

On Lincoln's career the speech had immediate effects. When the Republican national convention met less than a month later, more than a hundred votes were cast for Lincoln for the vice-presidential nomination. (He lost to William L. Dayton of New Jersey.) Lincoln became a national political figure because he had become a Republican party figure. From that year on, Lincoln stalked the presidency. He had never lacked self-confidence. Humility was his style but not his substance. He was now a sort of Messiah-in-waiting.

The political Lincoln had a regular companion in the Lincoln obliged to earn a living at the bar. Neither one blocked from public view the form and features of the other. There was the same ambition, the same thirst for admiration, the same casualness with the reputations of those who, for one cause or another, seemed to bar his way forward. Indeed, Lincoln's law practice was flourishing. The aforementioned Henry C. Whitney, an attorney for the Illinois Central Railroad, "never found him unwilling to appear in behalf of a great soul less [sic] corporation." Or against one. In a particular railroad case he earned a staggering, at the time, $5000 fee, which he duly split with his partner Herndon (who called him "purely and entirely a case lawyer," as distinguished from a lawyer with a prized specialty or a philosophical commitment).[55]

His sense of courtroom proprieties was, in the proper sense, Lincolnian. In one case Lincoln defended a man sued for damages for beating another man with a stick. Lincoln lampooned the accusation and attempted to show, through acting, that the injuries were trifling. His client had to pay only a small injury settlement.

Once he made fun of a man for calling himself J. Parker Green, using his middle name rather than his first name. (Lincoln himself, to be sure, had no middle name at all.)

Henry Clay Whitney, the amanuensis of Lincoln's Bloomington speech, was, like Lincoln, a lawyer. Indeed, he had traveled much with Lincoln on the circuit. He said that Lincoln always carried an air of superiority. He never lowered himself to the level of others. He said Lincoln was entertaining to a group yet never

---

[55] Wilson and Davis, p. 733; Donald, p. 156.

seemed to be of the group. He chose his companions as he did his reading — for utility, for what they could do for him.

History has pictured the lawyer Lincoln as defending the innocent, going about doing good, charging little or nothing. Examination proves him to have been not only a standard variety member of the Illinois bar but also an actor. He could be quite skillfully contemptuous, insulting, condescending, and aggressive, even to judges who let him get away with it.

On moral grounds he successfully defended some women who had emptied a saloon's whiskey barrels, portraying them as heroines making war on evil drink. The irony of the piece was that as a young man he had himself sold whiskey.

RIDING THE RISING TIDE

THE NEW POLITICAL PARTY he finally joined seemed in danger of not surviving the election of 1856. It had nominated John Charles Fremont as its presidential candidate. Its slogan was "Free Soil, Free Speech, and Fremont." The candidate was famous — an explorer, the "Conqueror of California" during the Mexican War. Moreover, he had married, in 1841, Jessie Benton, a daughter of the veteran Democratic Senator Thomas Hart Benton of Missouri. Although Benton, in a fascinating exercise of principle, opposed his son-in-law Fremont for the presidency, the family connection served him well enough. (For all that Fremont called himself by his middle name, "Charles," Lincoln spared him the ridicule he had visited upon J. Parker Green.).

When Lincoln came in second in the Republican balloting for vice-president, his friends were jubilant. He appeared to respond casually to the news, but the party's near-endorsement can only have gratified his ambition. He made more than 50 speeches during the campaign, attending meetings and barbeques. On the platform he said the election presented only one question — whether slavery should be allowed in the territories. "Buchanan says it shall, and Fremont says it shall not. That is the naked issue and the whole of it." He continued with the dubious assertion that if slaves were allowed in the new territories their value would double at once, a boon to Southerners interested in speculation of that kind. The other side was always evil.

Lincoln was working to make Illinois a Republican stronghold. He spoke of the South as unable to elect a Southern president, yet for all that, he said, vote-seeking Democrats catered to Southern wishes. He said, ludicrously, that the South controlled the U.S. government. The North was morally right, he insisted, and the South morally wrong. The South perforce had to yield.

The Republicans' candidate, Fremont, was glamorous, their platform stirring. But the new party, with its sectional nature and appeal, alarmed businessmen who had had no party since the Whigs died out. Most of these preferred the safe Buchanan to the reckless Fremont, who, if victorious, might indulge in rash acts that would precipitate disunion. In the end, Buchanan polled 174 electoral votes, Fremont 114, and Millard Fillmore, the candidate of the Know Nothing party, eight. The Democrats, with their supposed national appeal, would have lost but for the solid support they received in all the slave states except Maryland (which voted for Fillmore).

Fremont and Fillmore split the Old Whig vote, and Fremont's romantic but reckless image failed in comparison with those of two more stable candidates. In Illinois the new party swept the ticket, winning all the state offices. William Herndon got a job as state bank examiner, Lincoln a seat high in the party's councils.

As it happened, luck — or it may have been destiny — kissed the Republicans as they made way for the incoming government. Two days after Buchanan took office, the U.S. Supreme Court handed down a decision that would hasten the rush toward disunion. The case concerned a slave, Dred Scott, who had been taken by his master, an army surgeon, into Illinois, a free state, and Minnesota Territory, where slavery was forbidden under the Missouri Compromise. Scott, after the owner's death, sued in Missouri for freedom on that basis. The Supreme Court dismissed the case on the grounds, first, that a slave had no standing to bring suit in Missouri, hence in a federal court; and, second, that Congress, in the Missouri Compromise, had wrongly asserted power to prevent a citizen's right to carry any property, including slaves, into the territories. The Missouri Compromise was, accordingly, unconstitutional.

This decision cut the ground from under the positions both of the Republicans and of Stephen Douglas. The power to prohibit slavery in the territories was gone and, along with it, the doctrine of popular sovereignty. The Northern politicians and Northern press again went to work making the decision a cause célèbre, branding it a crime of the "Slave Power." If there was any conspiracy in the case it was on the other side — the suit was brought not for Scott's sake but for that of pure politics. (The former owner's widow had married an abolitionist who wished to press the courts for a decision strengthening the free soil position.)

Lincoln urged resistance to the decision, called it wrong, and accused Douglas, Chief Justice Roger B. Taney, and President Buchanan of a conspiracy. Lincoln spoke at a Republican banquet in Chicago in December 1857. He pointed to the rising tide of the party's power. He invited the members of the Free Soil party who had not already done so to leave their party and join the Republicans: "The human heart is with us; God is with us," he said. He criticized Buchanan for being 200,000 votes short of a popular majority. (He himself would become president three years later with less than 40 percent of the popular vote.)

The slavery issue was growing like a malignancy now, seizing upon the interest of people previously indifferent. "Slavery extension," theoretical as it was, became an important subject to everybody.

Douglas said the Dred Scott decision was law and should be followed. Lincoln said it was wrong and ought to be overruled.

Although the institution of slavery was on the defensive as never before, Lincoln gave an emotional address to the effect that slaves were being tormented as never before. Douglas said that Lincoln's program would produce a race problem, that blacks would vote, eat, sleep, and marry with whites. Lincoln scoffed at such an assertion. Douglas spoke of Lincoln's constant extraction from the Declaration of Independence of the phrase "all men are created equal." Douglas said that the sentence meant that a British subject on the American continent was politically equal to British subjects in Great Britain, that it did not refer to Negroes and was no injunction to mandate Negro equality. Lincoln said that Douglas's interpretation would mean that all other white people in the world were inferior, a spurious conclusion that he could hardly believe himself. It was a lawyer's response. It seemed to answer; in fact, it was no answer at all.

Of Douglas's statement that Lincoln's program would end in the creation of a mixed race, Lincoln said the thought horrified him. He then blamed the existence of mulattoes on slave masters who supposedly forced black women into concubinage. He claimed that his measures would bring about less, not more race mixing.[56]

The luck of the Republicans had no end, it seemed. In 1857 a financial panic occurred. In rapidly growing states such as Illinois, living on credit, capital-hungry, thirsting for the government subsidy that always dries up at such times, the reaction was particularly strong. This panic gave the Republicans a second issue. The United States government was in the hands of a Democratic administration, a low-tariff regime; the Old Whigs who had become Republicans knew how to preach their old cure-all, a high tariff. This would damage President

---

[56] Sandburg, Vol. 2, p. 94.

Buchanan in his own industrialized state, Pennsylvania. Powerful capitalists could be enticed by tariff and other pocketbook issues into backing a party whose social and constitutional doctrines were revolutionary.

As for the social doctrines, the 21st century pays no attention to the contradictions — by 21st century standards — in Lincoln's views of racial questions. His disdain for "amalgamation" of the white and black races is slightly better publicised than his support for repatriation of the slaves to Africa — a cause that Henry Clay himself had embraced. "It was Lincoln's opinion," writes the Lincoln scholar Harry V. Jaffa, "as it was Thomas Jefferson's, that the only natural right which the Negro possessed which required civil recognition, beyond emancipation, was the right to emigrate."[57]

An idea much abroad at the time in the North as well as the South was that freed slaves could be resettled in or much nearer their homelands. John G. Nicolay and John Hay wrote that "Without being an enthusiast, he [Lincoln] was a firm believer in colonization." Indeed, in 1857, he was elected a manager of the Illinois State Colonization Society, an organisation directed to the cause of resettlement. Orville H. Browning was president. John Randolph of Roanoke 30 years before had called the notion "a foolish, impractical endeavor," but people North and South had supported it. Whatever success might have come of the venture had not war intervened in 1861, not a tithe of a tenth of the national yearly increase in Negro population was ever exported.[58]

---

[57] Harry V. Jaffa, *Crisis of the House Divided*, University of Chicago Press, 1999.

[58] Nicolay and Hay, Vol. 6, pp. 354-55.

In 1858, the capital of Kansas Territory was the town of Lecompton. A pro-Southern territorial legislature seated there, and probably representing a majority of the bona fide settlers in Kansas, submitted to the U.S. Congress what was called the "Lecompton Constitution." It represented the attempt of the Southern party in the territory to salvage something out of the wreck of pro-slavery hopes. It had become evident that hopes of a permanent addition of Kansas to the roster of slave states were vain. But framers of the Lecompton Constitution hoped to protect the property rights of the few slaveholders in Kansas and to try to elect two senators from what would be nominally a slave state. It was purely a question of principle, because Southerners knew that immigration and economics showed that Kansas would never be permanently a slave state. Once admitted as a state, Kansas would be free to abolish slavery at any time. The Lecompton Constitution paid respect to "popular sovereignty" as it allowed the settlers to vote on slavery. But it did not allow them to vote on the new constitution apart from slavery. President Buchanan and the leaders of the Democratic party accepted the Lecompton Constitution as a convenient way to end the territorial controversy that had been sapping the energy of the nation for four years. The United States had other matters to worry about. Let Kansas be admitted and the affair closed so the nation could attend to more important concerns. It was hoped that the new Constitution might complete such pacifying work as the Dred Scott decision might yet achieve by clarifying at least the highly ambiguous position of slavery in the territories.

These hopes were not unreasonable, but the Republicans were. Peace would have damaged them, perhaps forever. Their political life had begun with the Kansas controversy and might end with it. The Free Soilers had boycotted the election in Kansas for delegates to a constitutional convention. They regarded (unreasonably, as it happened) the territorial governor, Robert J. Walker, as a stooge for the Buchanan administration. If Kansas were admitted to the Union, the Republicans could not keep the pot boiling forever. Sooner or later the heat would simmer down, and the Democrats might win.

Again the Republicans were lucky. Every time the water returned to a simmer, something occurred to save them. This time it was Stephen Douglas himself who stirred up the pot. Apostles and apologists for Lincoln have often over the years blackened the name of Douglas along with the names of Mary Todd Lincoln, Gen. George B. McClellan, anti-war Northerners, Southerners as a class, and most of Lincoln's generals, predecessors, competitors, and successors. If Douglas had been no more than a power-hungry politician, he would never have stepped in to stir up the dying fire in Kansas. He had introduced the Kansas-Nebraska bill in sincerity, at great risk to himself, assuring the nation that he had no desire to aid or hinder slavery, asserting that he was merely putting into effect the old Democratic doctrine of majority rule. Now he saw his promises going away by the action of the Lecompton party in Kansas, and in the hasty acceptance of their constitution by President Buchanan.

Buchanan formally asked Douglas to follow the President. Douglas refused. The Democrats were fragmenting.

The Republicans were coalescing. Lincoln was now the foremost of the Illinois politicians contributing to it. He was a party man, in the middle of party affairs, constantly communicating with party leaders around the state. He observed every caucus: precinct, city, county, or congressional district. He spent hours daily figuring ballots, candidates, tickets. He knew all the political devices. He knew hundreds of precinct and county workers ready for appointment as clerk, postmaster, magistrate, or any other office if victory was won. Months before a candidate or a potential appointee would be nominated, Lincoln would have appraised him carefully. He was involved in every aspect of party work.

He neglected his law practice for politics, admitting to this dereliction in answer to a client's question of why he was not progressing on a case. He wrote hundreds of letters to party workers. He converted the German immigrant population to Republicanism.

Buchanan reminded Douglas of the fall from power of eminent Democrats who had differed with Buchanan's old boss, President Andrew Jackson. The separation into a Douglas faction and a Buchanan faction drove a wedge right through the middle of the Democratic party, making Lincoln's victory two years later all but inevitable. The divorce of Van Buren Democrats from Polk Democrats a decade earlier was the first wound.

Opposing Lecompton, Douglas had now managed to alienate the South, having long before alienated the professional structure of his own party. He knew it, but he stood for principle. Lincoln would never have made that mistake. He never let principle defeat policy. But Douglas hurt himself, and he knew it. Douglas was still the most powerful man in politics with the average, ordinary voter. When the Republicans compared his strength with their poor showing against Buchanan in 1856, many of them decided they should join forces with him and guarantee a victory. Either leave him a free field in his senatorial campaign of 1858 or give him outright support that would defeat the regular Democrats — such were the strategic choices. Douglas might even join their party. If that should occur, then the Republicans would certainly win the presidency in 1860. Horace Greeley in the *New York Tribune* was a great favourite of Illinois farmers. He liked this approach. So did Republicans in New York and Boston.

But standing in the way of this strategy was the political ambition of Abraham Lincoln.

Lincoln saw the notice; the attention Douglas would confer on a political opponent. A challenger in the ring with the champion has all eyes riveted upon him. Schisms were opening everywhere. All of them served to injure Douglas. Many conservative Whigs who had refused to follow Lincoln into the Republican Party in 1856 were ready to support him as Douglas, never a Whig to begin with, was now regarded as a disturber of the peace in Kansas. If both Lincoln and Douglas were going to share the radical views of the eastern "Black Republicans" who kept stirring up the slavery issue, then it would be better to support Lincoln as he was the weaker of the two, and therefore able to do less harm.

Had it not been for Lincoln's personal ambition, Douglas and the Republicans would have made some sort of common cause. Such was not to be. Just as the Republican party generally wanted to divide the Douglas Democrats from the Buchanan Democrats, and wanted to insure party victory by joining their forces to Douglas, Lincoln wanted to split the Illinois Republicans from the Eastern Republicans. Lincoln and his backers began to tell the local Republicans why they should not let the eastern "Black Republicans" have their evil way.

Douglas's stand against the Lecompton Constitution had made him unpopular in the South. Would it take votes from Lincoln now that Douglas's position was similar to his? Not many votes, Lincoln suspected. Party feeling was too high, and Douglas's profile had been prominent so long that he had made plenty of political enemies. Besides, Lincoln could afford to lose some votes. There were plenty of new ones to harvest. Illinois was filling up with immigrants. From 1850 to 1860, the state's population more than doubled. Immigrants from the east and from Europe accounted for two-thirds of the increase. These were grist for the Republican mill. Many were Irish; others were Germans unable even to speak English. Lincoln bought a German-language newspaper, the *Illinois Staats Anzeiger*,[59] and went to work telling its readers that they were common people, subject to being enslaved by Southern aristocrats. The immigrants were solid for the new party. Illinois had originally been settled by the Southern-born like Lincoln himself. Those people were Democrats and old-line Whigs — an entirely different constituency from the newcomers.

Lincoln spent the spring of 1858 writing a speech. He was going to be nominated by his party for senator from Illinois. He accused President Pierce, President Buchanan, Chief Justice Taney, and Senator Douglas of conspiracy. History has shown that there was no conspiracy, except on the other side — Lincoln's own. Lincoln forecast that the Supreme Court would make Illinois a slave state. It was a ridiculous charge, one he could hardly have believed himself. He charged conspiracy but was careful not to use the word. He was an abolitionist but careful not to admit it.

The Republicans nailed together a skillful platform. The German vote was cemented by the election of Gustave Koerner as president of the convention. Koerner, a German immigrant and a former Democrat, had served as lieutenant governor, becoming state Republican party chairman in 1856. His influence with the Germans of Illinois was large. The tariff issue was ignored. Eastern Republican manufacturers wanted the tariff. The Midwestern Republicans, caring less about the issue, left it alone. Their platform was general, vague, safe.

---

[59] Donald, p. 242.

Lincoln addressed the convention at Springfield on June 16, 1858. In his now-perfected serious, quiet style he spoke of slavery as a moral wrong. He avoided specifics and was able to avoid antagonising any of the Illinois voters. He used general moralizing to cover his refusal to endanger himself by the use of specifics.[60] A central passage e in the speech, paraphrasing words of Jesus in the Gospel of Mark, became famous, and has remained so: "A house divided against itself cannot stand. I believe this government cannot endure permanently half slave and half free. I do not expect the Union to be dissolved" — this to quickly assure the voters that the Republicans, the party of disunion, was not the party of disunion. "I do not expect the house to fall, but I do expect it will cease to be divided. It will become all one thing or another."

This qualified as news. The house in question had endured under one form of government or another — colonial, revolutionary, constitutional — and in its "divided" configuration for more than two centuries. What had changed so suddenly to indicate that Americans could not continue to accommodate their differences? Accommodation of differences was the whole basis of the federal system. The founding fathers had provided in 1787 for a federal rather than a consolidated power structure. The Constitution contained important checks against the assertion of disproportionate power by any faction or region. As Professor Forrest McDonald has wisely noted, "The Founding Fathers believed that men in government must be regarded as driven by unbounded lust for power and profit .... From this it followed that powers must be so distributed that people who are vested with them at any level have an interest in

---

[60] Lincoln, *Speeches and Writings*, Vol. 1., pp. 426-434.

curbing the powers of all others." [61] Midway through the 19th century, the cantons of Switzerland arrived at the same understanding and contrived their own version of federalism. Both America and Switzerland were, and remain, nations of diverse elements: diverse in climate, people, economies, and religion. The Swiss have held fast to that principle. The Americans have abandoned it.

Hardly anyone expected slavery to flourish in Kansas or Nebraska. It had not amounted to much even in Missouri. But Lincoln took the position that allowing a slaveowner to enter Kansas meant denying the rights of the free men. Illinois had banned immigration of Negroes, slave or free. The Northern population did not want Negro immigration into their states. Lincoln told his audiences that the whites would be enslaved next — the basis of his feverish accusation that Douglas, Presidents Pierce and Buchanan, and Chief Justice Taney were party to a conspiracy to make the free states slave states, thus taking jobs away from the white man. This alarmed the simple, and especially newly-arrived immigrants. Lincoln was seeking to alarm, not to calm. He aimed at discord, not harmony. Careers are not made from concord.

"Honest Abe" had not yet been given that name. That sobriquet would come via the political bosses, wishing to distinguish the western "honest pioneer" from the "corrupt" politicians in the East. "Honest Abe," who was if nothing else a man of remarkable intelligence, certainly knew better. He was uttering demagogy clothed in Biblical language. His "house divided" speech was just

---

[61] Edward B. McLean, *Derailing the Constitution: The Undermining of American Federalism*, introduction by Forrest McDonald, Intercollegiate Studies Institute, 1995, p. 36.

the kind of speech a rising political party liked to hear. He did not commit himself to any dangerous policy.

Lincoln talked to the Buchanan Democrats, encouraging them to run independently of Douglas. Douglas had plenty of problems, having alienated both sides on the issue, as well as his own president. Furthermore, he was opposed by a party seeking power, and seeking to get it by means of the Midwesterner's wish to keep out the Negro.

Douglas knew he had problems, but he also had courage. He did not back away, but attacked Lincoln on specifics. In Chicago, on July 9, 1858, he said the "House Divided" speech was an invitation to disunion, as well as an attack on local liberty. He accused Lincoln of advocating "a war of the North against the South, a war of extermination until one or the other shall be subdued and all the states shall either become free or become slave."[62] It was an accurate prediction. Douglas said that Lincoln's unitary conception would mean that the United States would have to have whiskey prohibition everywhere or nowhere. He said that under Lincoln the Union would become "one consolidated empire." Not only did the Republicans assail the rights of the states, he said, but their attacks on the Supreme Court over the Dred Scott decision were endangering "our rights, our property, and our liberty." Finally, he charged that the Republican insistence on the rights of the black man endangered the rights of the white men for whom and by whom the government was made. The whole enterprise would end in political and racial amalgamation.

Lincoln denied all Douglas's accusations, but his answers avoided detail and remained metaphysical and non-specific. He

---

[62] Donald, p. 210.

spent the next two years skillfully denying the same points. He scoffed at the idea that he was after destroying the Union, destroying the South — all the rest of it. Yet everything Douglas accused him of he did, and worse, and did immediately upon taking up the presidency.

It is interesting and necessary in appraising Lincoln to compare what he said with what he did, his words with his deeds. It is interesting to read how he said one thing to one audience and denied it to another.

Douglas raised specific questions. Lincoln gave general answers, resorting to abstract references to the Declaration of Independence. It is hard to pin down an abstraction, and Lincoln remained abstract. Lincoln's words were pretty but were pure lawyer's cant. Douglas said that Lincoln's talk of a "house divided" was mere talk, rash and violent. (The South certainly took it that way.) Lincoln replied that division was not his wish, merely an impending reality to which he had to call attention. (As president two years later, he fulfilled that supposed reality by going to war, on his own initiative, within a few weeks of taking office.) He called slavery a moral question but brushed aside consideration of practical approaches to resolution of that question. Douglas, by contrast, was honestly looking for real-world solutions. Lincoln asserted the right to refuse obedience to the Dred Scott decision. He said the court could change its mind and "we mean to do what we can to have the court decide the other way."

He accused Douglas of being indifferent to the principles of the Declaration of Independence ("all men are created equal"), saying that his opponent threatened the liberties of white immigrants as well as black men. At no time did he even address himself to the practical results of his preaching.

The Republicans were men of various stripes: a motley group of anti-Democrats, joined by a common need for a power vehicle, meaning a political party. Unable to control the Democratic party, they undertook to manufacture a political grouping of their own. George Fitzhugh of Virginia, who decried the abolitionist enterprise in two widely read books of the 1850s, said that he worked to warn the North that the abolitionists stood for revolution, that Northern private property, churches, laws and marriages would be swept out in flames if the abolitionists should have their way. To language and prophecies of this sort the North's intensifying campaign against slavery was driving many Southerners, making compromise and concession virtual impossibilities.

THE BIGGEST STAGE OF ALL

AFTER THE CHICAGO SPEECHES, Lincoln and Douglas continued in the same vein, adding nothing of substantive worth. Lincoln was full of anecdotes, metaphors and metaphysics; Douglas, by contrast, searched for solutions and looked to the real world. He continued to assert that he had defended self-government in 1854 against the passions of the North; now he was defending it against the passions of the South. Douglas said that Lincoln's attitude was incompatible with the peace of the Union and with the supremacy of the white race. Lincoln might say that he meant only to preserve for the Negro the right to "life, liberty and the pursuit of happiness" asserted in the Declaration of Independence as the natural rights of every man. The result of his quest, nevertheless, would be the destruction of free government and the undermining of basic rights supposedly sacred to the country's European founders.

Lincoln denied that he was allied with the Buchanan Democrats against Douglas. He said over and over that the Dred Scott decision was a conspiracy to force slavery upon all the states, and that Stephen Douglas was part of the conspiracy. The fact has been confirmed ever since by every study that if there was a conspiracy it was on the other side.

Democratic newspapers derided Lincoln for his fake humility, called him a "Uriah Heep" after the Character in Dickens's *David Copperfield* who continually asserts his supposedly humble character, all the while meditating malice and treachery. Lincoln stated in his speeches that he did not believe Negroes to be the equal of whites and that he was unwilling to have them vote or be made citizens in Illinois.[63]

The campaign reached its peak in the series of seven debates between the two titans of the 1850s controversies, Lincoln and Douglas. Douglas was seeking re-election to the Senate; Lincoln offered himself for the post. To gain the attention that sharing a platform with Douglas would give him, Lincoln asked for debates. Douglas — unwisely, as would be seen — accepted. The challenger in such affairs is always the lesser known candidate seeking attention, so Lincoln had everything to gain, whereas the incumbent, Douglas, had everything to lose and nothing to gain.

Lincoln was a skillful talker, and Douglas knew it. He said himself that if Lincoln out-talked him, "I shall lose everything." But Douglas never refused a fight.

The debates demonstrated the style of each man. Douglas talked without jests, anecdotes, or abstractions. He treated the issues in terms of practical, factual requirements. Lincoln remained general, non-specific, metaphysical, abstract, remote, humorous, anecdotal and conversational in style. He was a professional common man in public presentations, though aloof and proud: aware of his own importance when not on stage. He was successful. He acquitted himself well, although his speeches read best in excerpts due to their moralistic and abstract style. Lincoln spoke on both sides of issues, contradicting himself whenever he thought it necessary. Twenty-five years of practice, of dedication to the art of persuasion, added to a natural talent with words, made Lincoln a skilled declaimer. Poetry spoken does not make the speaker virtuous. Lord Byron soared to the heavens when it

---

[63] Lincoln, *A Documentary Portrait*, p. 5.

came to imagery but descended to hell when it came to personal practice.

Throughout his career Lincoln's speeches and public utterances, marked by ambiguous rhetoric and eloquent digression, and skillful appeals to religion and current dogma, distracted the attention of his hearers from the various real points at issue. Douglas, on the other hand, stuck to the question.

The two men were an arresting contrast in styles and outlooks — Douglas blunt and earnest, Lincoln far the craftier of the two, keeping his own counsel, hiding with some skill certain attributes his hearers might resist and resent. Upon his nature he superimposed what he presented as a preference for the common man. He worked at that public image and never failed to accuse his opponents of aristocracy, privilege, and base motives. He was thus a standard politician. Lincoln had been called the rich man's politician by members of his own party. He had defended himself publicly from the charge. On the other hand, he never shrank from the making of money, or from service to the cause of the moneymen who sought government intervention — i.e., tariffs, land giveaways and railroad and mining subsidies — to feather their own nests.

As for Douglas — Lincoln's rhetoric aside — he had had a harder childhood and a more genuine struggle than had Lincoln. Lincoln's father was easy, indulgent. Douglas's step-father had abused him. In his speeches Douglas was far more candid and in his relations with other people quite kind, more generous and less aloof than the demanding Lincoln. But Lincoln was more skillful in communicating his common man image to the average voter. It was a feat of acting. As an orator Lincoln was the equal of any, if not the superior. Oratory is always acting: a very demanding form because the actor must write most of his own lines. Lincoln's style was no longer bombastic and shrill. He had learned, from Calhoun, the power of a quiet tone.

The Lincoln-Douglas debates have been extracted from reality, made out to be both important and dramatic. Thus, they are part of American legend. The fact was, they did give Lincoln, the challenger, needed public attention. They were not, for all that, an event that revealed Lincoln as Douglas's superior. Both men did well. The legend is that Lincoln showed himself noble, honest, and farsighted, whereas Douglas was cunning and evasive. That opinion is myth. Lincoln did succeed in pushing Douglas further into the hole that the territory conflict had opened. At Freeport, he asked Douglas, "Can the people of a Territory exclude slavery from its borders?"[64] In other words, was popular sovereignty still a legal formula, the Supreme Court's decision in the Dred Scott case notwithstanding? The question was a trap. No matter how Douglas replied — and well Lincoln knew it — he was sure to offend. He stood his ground anyway. Slavery indeed could be excluded from a new territory through its legislature's failure to enact laws protecting it. His answer had the inevitable effect of alienating opinion both in the North and the South. The former desired a more moralistic stance on slavery, the latter an affirmation of the South's right not to be excluded from the territories. Southerners called Douglas' reply the "Freeport Heresy" and likened it to betrayal.

Lincoln's associates had advised him not to ask that question as it would not help him in Illinois. Lincoln returned, in essence, that voter irritation of a temporary nature was a small price to pay for a coup that could open the way to the White House.

---

[64] For text of the debates, Lincoln, *Speeches and Writings*, Vol. 1, pp. 537-580.

His close allies knew the presidency was his real aim. Lincoln knew that Douglas had been forced into a position that would split the Democratic party and kill Douglas's own chances of election to the presidency.

Shortly after the debates had concluded, a speech far more important to Lincoln's nomination was made, but by neither Lincoln nor Douglas. Senator William Seward of New York, the most prominent national figure after Douglas, and the man expected to be nominated by the Republicans for president, spoke at Rochester, New York, on October 25. His speech had more force in propelling Lincoln to the presidency than any Lincoln himself ever made. Of the sectional controversy that seemed to portend disunion, Seward said, "Shall I tell you what this collision means? ... It is an irrepressible conflict between opposing and enduring forces, and it means that the United States must and will sooner or later, become either entirely a slaveholding nation or entirely a free-labor nation." That slavery would spread throughout the nation was impossible. That slavery would return to the Middle Atlantic or New England states was a prospect in which no one believed, South or North. No Southerner ever contended that slavery was anything except a state matter. The South was merely trying to hold on to its ancient estate, but the Republicans needed the issue to advance their cause.[65]

In proclaiming the "irrepressible conflict," Seward was repeating Republican doctrine, inflaming the issue just as Lincoln had. But Lincoln, at the time of his house-divided speech, had been too obscure a figure for the warning to resonate. Seward, by contrast, was too prominent for his words to die away unnoticed.

---

[65] Glyndon G. Van Duesen, *William Henry Seward*, Oxford University Press, 1967, p. 193.

Conservative Americans were rightly alarmed. Here was a Republican saying exactly what their opponents accused him of saying — namely, that Republicans were the party of one issue, one section; the party of division, strife, and disunion. No presidential candidate promises war: not Franklin Roosevelt, not Woodrow Wilson, not George W. Bush, not even Lincoln.

Not just the South, but also the Northern Democrats, the ordinary Americans, the more conservative Republicans, and even the party managers were alarmed. Seward was regarded as dangerous, his candidacy a threat to survival of the young Republican party. Republicans could not afford a candidate who would alarm the electorate and almost kill the party as the impulsive Fremont had done in 1856.

By the time of Seward's speech in late October the Illinois senatorial campaign was all but over. Douglas had turned his bad position at the beginning into victory at the end. The Republicans elected the governor, the legislature had a small Democrat majority to elect a Senator, and Douglas saved his hide. Outside the South, Douglas was the idol of the Democrats. The Buchanan faction was weak and reduced in number.

Lincoln had lost again. He had a long string of losses. He had lost in Congress; despite the victory of Zachary Taylor in 1848, he had failed to get a good government job offer; he had lost for the Senate against Trumbull in a bitter defeat in 1854. And now Douglas had beaten him.

But this time Lincoln was in a good mood. Even in losing, he could see that his life was taking a new turn. The campaign had made his reputation. The human flame that was Douglas had lighted up, inadvertently, his opponent. Lincoln's name was now familiar to the voters all over the country. The Republican party was grateful to Lincoln because his running against Douglas had strengthened the party, perhaps saved it by his careful campaign.

Lincoln was now in demand as a speaker. He was a name within the party, not as high a one as Seward and Chase, but in the next rank, certainly. Second rank might be an advantage. Every president since Jackson had come from the second rank of his party, overcoming such as Henry Clay, Daniel Webster, and John C. Calhoun. Political parties like victory. It began to occur to the Republicans that Chase and Seward and Sumner might not win, that a better candidate might be one not so strongly identified or stigmatized as a fanatic. Lincoln's presidential ambitions, now apparent to his associates, were put resolutely to work.

Lincoln knew what he wanted and went out to get it.

For the next two years his was an extensive and intensive pursuit of the big prize. Wanting to advertise himself in the East, he took a trip to Exeter, New Hampshire, where his son Robert, a laggard student, was enrolled in the famous preparatory school. He arranged to be invited to address a great public meeting of the Republican party in New York. Eleven years earlier, he had spoken for Zachary Taylor in the East. Then he was an obscure Whig party member; now he was a well-known Republican party leader.

At New York City's Cooper Union, on February 27, 1860 — three months in advance of the Republican presidential convention — he delivered the speech that may have assured him of that convention's nomination. Somber clouds overhung the national skies as Lincoln, an essentially local figure, rose to address an audience of the nationally lustrous. Only four months earlier, the Kansas renegade John Brown, financed by wealthy New York and New England abolitionists, had tried to incite a slave rebellion by seizing the federal arsenal at Harpers Ferry, Virginia. The government quickly broke the Brown uprising (in which not a single slave took part), tried the bearded, wild-eyed leader for treason, and in a matter of a few weeks hanged him. As Lincoln spoke, two members of the Brown gang awaited their own executions.

The South was duly fearful of what blow might next descend from an unexpected quarter upon its security and standing in the Union. Days earlier, Senator Jefferson Davis of Mississippi had introduced a set of resolutions meant to safeguard the full exercise of a Southern right to make determinate judgments respecting slavery. Throughout the South, legislators and leaders were tuning up to call for secession in the event of a Republican presidential victory in November.

Lincoln, at Cooper Union, portrayed with some show of personal reluctance his intention not to interfere with slavery where it existed already. As for its expansion into the territories, here he drew the line. The founding fathers, he said, would never have assented to such a prospect. The assertion was a venture in question-begging. Helpless to prove such a point — what had the founders thought about territory the nation had not yet acquired? — Lincoln threw his long, lank arm around them as one distinguished body, congratulating them on seeing things his way. His foray into historical speculation enabled him to claim that opposition to popular sovereignty was a conservative, not a radical, expedient. Yet the "conservative" Lincoln rejected "groping for some middle ground between the right and the wrong ... such as a policy of 'don't care' on a question about which all true men do care." It was a glove across the face of Stephen A. Douglas, this imputation that popular sovereignty meant indifference to matters of right and wrong. Lincoln continued: "Neither let us be slandered from our duty by false accusations against us, nor frightened from it by menaces of destruction to the Government nor of dungeons to ourselves. Let us have faith that right makes might, and in that faith, let us, to the end, dare to do our duty as we understand it."[66]

The speech made a considerable sensation: firmness without bellicosity; intellectual as well as rhetorical eloquence. As it was, Lincoln's political prospects were growing. Expectations were that Illinois, at the convention, would put him forward as a "favorite son." His political friends had stronger plans. Lincoln had many assets. He was not prominent enough as a Republican to frighten the voters who looked upon the party as the intemperate sectional party of dis-union and violence likely to start a war. He had had too brief and too obscure a role to have made enemies. He could be portrayed as a common man (even though he had a son at Phillips Exeter).

He could be represented as a poor boy — a good choice to exploit the charge that the South was aristocratic. He could make the Republican party (the party of the powerful commercial and manufacturing interests) appeal to the common man. Dennis Hanks had found some rails that he claimed that Lincoln had split thirty years before. The rail-splitter image (upon the smooth lawyer) was as irrelevant as William Henry Harrison's log cabin, but it would serve the purpose.

An appealing image would not be quite enough. The professional politicians, not the people, did the nominating. They prized the popular appeal Lincoln was capable of displaying — wit, intelligence, and with it a certain everydayness. But first the candidate had to convince the party professionals that he had what they wanted. Lincoln's group, like Lincoln himself, were professionals — masters of behind-the-scene electioneering. For

---

[66] Lincoln, *Speeches and Writings*, Vol. 2, pp. 111-130.

two years Lincoln and his faction were never still, never missing an opportunity.

The convention met in Chicago on May 16, 1860. The race pitted William H. Seward against the field. Lincoln's group decided to run against Seward, to focus on the resentments and fears Seward's prominence aroused. They described Lincoln as representing the "little" interests against the "big" ones. Held in Lincoln's home state, the convention afforded Lincoln particular advantages. He was able to pack the galleries with noisy and organised supporters bearing counterfeit admission tickets. The Lincolnites were able to exclude Seward's supporters from entrance. An important order of business was the promising of cabinet seats in exchange for delivery of certain states' votes. This duly accomplished, Lincoln won nomination on the third ballot. Henry Whitney saw Lincoln's victory as the product of political skill, overlain with political genius. The man whose account of the Bloomington speech alone gives some sense of that occasion speculated that the experience might have awakened in Lincoln the desire to compete for the country's paramount political office.

True enough, following the convention he returned home, telling Mary, his wife, that, barring some unlikely event, he would be the next president of the United States. In fact, he was deservedly gloomy about the outcome. The country was more than divided: it was rent asunder. A second Democratic convention had to be held in Baltimore, following the party's initial failure, in Charleston, to muster a two-thirds majority for Douglas. It was a tired and dispirited party that finally placed its gigantic bet on the Little Giant. The Southern Democrats were unappeased. They met in Richmond and nominated John C. Breckinridge of Kentucky. That was not even the end of it. A convention of former Southern Whigs, at about the same time as the Republican convention, formed the Constitutional Union party and nominated for president U.S. Senator John Bell of Tennessee and for vice-president Edward Everett of Massachusetts (the orator whose remarks, three years later, at Gettysburg, would precede the president's more widely remembered words). The party's moderate tone and ambiguous platform seemed designed for purposes of throwing the election into the House of Representatives, where cooler, conservative heads might — might! — prevail. The same party feuds that had endangered Douglas's senatorial election — more bitter now than before; more divisive — conspired to deny him the presidential office he might have used to chain the dogs of war.

Lincoln's nomination, despite what his biographers have said, startled the country, and frightened the more sober members even of his own party. They knew how the South feared him; they knew a crisis, worse perhaps than that of 1850, was approaching. They knew that Lincoln had no practice at administration, nor any liking or talent for it. His sole experience above the state legislative level, was one undistinguished term in the House of Representatives. He was an unknown. All he had manifested was political ambition — a lust for power. What would he do when all that power was his?

Yet who at this point could stand against him?

Stephen A. Douglas campaigned vigorously, including in the South. On November 2, on the steps of the state capitol at Montgomery, Alabama, though addressing an audience whose views opposed his, Douglas was candid, honest, objective, factual, stating the problem. What he said here was consistent with what he said elsewhere. It is a typical sample of his speeches, whether given North or South. It stands in stark contrast to Lincoln's vague, evasive, dissembling speeches, whose meaning was deliberately veiled, permitting of various interpretations, politically allowing Lincoln to appear uncommitted; demagogic, while seeming mild; poetic, metaphysical, abstract, epigrammatic while inviting public action against the supposedly immoral South. Lincoln's speeches were poetry; Douglas's were prose. Douglas suggested how the effects of the storm gathering over the young, untried republic might have been suppressed, given some luck, time, and good will. The Little Giant as it happened was not the future that lay in store for America. Lincoln — all rhetoric, all stately meter, with religious and philosophical borrowings — was the future.

COLD IN CRISIS

Men of ambition, in pursuit of glory, thirsting for distinction, do spring up. Such men will have it, whether at the expense of emancipating slaves or enslaving free men. When such a one does, it will require the people to be united, attached to the laws, to successfully frustrate his designs.[67]
- Abraham Lincoln, Springfield Lyceum, 27 January 1838

THE MOST IMPORTANT ELECTION ever held in the United States of America took place on November 3, 1860. Abraham Lincoln was elected president. He, one man, would destroy a form of government based on centuries of Anglo-European thought, derived from Greco-Roman philosophy and shaped by 253 years of hard-earned American experience that began at Jamestown, Virginia, in 1607. For 253 years America had prospered under a system of limited government. That edifice was to be brought down and replaced by a consolidated, centralised power.

Lincoln was the only purely sectional president the United States had ever had. Lincoln, the Republican, received almost a million votes fewer than the two Democratic candidates, Douglas and Breckinridge, out of 4.7 million votes cast altogether. In the entire Midwest Lincoln's majority was only 6,600. A change of one vote in 20 would have given the Midwest to Douglas and sent the election (consonant with the likely hopes of the Constitutional

---

[67] *Ibid.*, pp. 28-36.

Union party) to the House of Representatives, where Douglas would presumably have been elected. In 15 states Lincoln did not receive a single electoral vote; in 10 — all of them Southern — he received not one single popular vote. The ordinary citizens cared little for him. But for the abolitionists, the enormous number of recent immigrants, and certain monied interests in the Northeastern states, he would have lost anyway. The Republicans won the North because the Democratic party, even there, was split into factions. He failed to carry his own Sangamon County. None of the Lincolns, and only one of the Hankses, voted for him. The Congressional election had produced a large majority opposed to the Republican platform. The Republican Party had its weaknesses.

But the Democrats had committed political suicide, splitting their vote two ways, between Senator Douglas and Vice-President Breckinridge. The Constitutional Union party siphoned off 589,000 votes, an impressive total for a party bent mainly on keeping things as they were. The Democrats were doomed before election day. Most knew, or at any rate sensed, the Republican nominee would win. His victory was purely the result of Democratic factionalism, North and South. The electorate knew Lincoln would win. The nervous uncertainty was that nobody knew what he would do.

Southerners and Democrats complained that the nation would be ruled by a sectional minority. That minority now had the power and was ready to work its will. The South had been waiting in dread for the inevitable calamity. Immediately, several states began talking secession. In his pre-election speeches Lincoln had scoffed at the suggestion that his election would cause such an effect. He did not want Northern voters to know what he knew, and what the South knew — namely, that his assumption of the presidency was a credible threat to the Union he talked so much about wishing to preserve. As day succeeded day after the election, and Lincoln spoke nothing conciliatory, setting a cold distance between himself and those seeking assurance that peace might prevail, the South felt its fears confirmed.

Those fears were accompanied by some astonishment at being notified that the door into the Union seemed to have been shut and bolted behind its members: prisoners in their own national home, it seemed. What was the basis of such a claim? Alexis de Tocqueville, in *Democracy in America*, noting the "voluntary agreement" that had produced the Union, held that "If one of the States chose to withdraw its name from the contract, it would be difficult to disprove its right of doing so; and the Federal Government would have no means of maintaining its claims directly, either by force or by right."[68] Had there ever been a more ardent advocate of centralised government than Alexander Hamilton? The same Hamilton instructed his fellow delegates to the constitutional convention that "To coerce the States is one of the maddest projects that was ever devised …."[69] Even the Federalists of Massachusetts, during the War of 1812, had claimed the right of secession. New York specifically reserved that right when it ratified the Constitution and joined the Union. John Quincy Adams, ardent foe of slavery, had argued in 1839 that states alienated from one another by "cold indifference, or collision of interests" should "part in friendship from each other"

---

[68] Alexis de Tocqueville, *Democracy in America*, 2 vols., Arlington House, 1966, p. 381.

[69] Thomas J. DiLorenzo, *Real Lincoln*, pp. 89-90.

rather than "be held together by constraint."[70] The South never questioned its right to withdraw from a compact that had become unfriendly to the region's society. Lincoln's position daily increased Southern belief that secession was necessary.

On the South's reading of the situation, the threats hurled its way for so long would now become deeds. In Lincoln's election the extreme anti-South faction had gained control of the mighty federal power. Two political observers of diametrically opposite orientations saw the matter the same way. Both Karl Marx and Britain's prime minister, Lord Palmerston, said that the South had lost the right to control its own affairs.

The South now had to decide what to do.

In the South there were now only two views. The majority in the Lower South felt that leaving the Union was the only way to end constant abuse and threats from the North. The other group opposed secession, relying upon diplomacy and negotiation, believing the South would be better able to defend itself within the Union than out of it. Some Southern Whigs and some Democrats argued this. One fact was certain: From the Potomac to the Rio Grande, no pro-Lincoln faction existed. All knew that the power of the sword, and the desire to wield it, lay in Lincoln's party only. All the South wanted was "to be let alone."[71]

Jefferson Davis and Alexander Stephens, the future president and vice-president of the Southern Confederacy, wished that the

---

[70] *Ibid.*, p. 88.

[71] To the Confederate Congress, April 29, Davis said, "All we ask is to be let alone – that those who never held power over us shall not now attempt our subjugation by arms." Hudson Strode, *Jefferson Davis: Confederate President*, Harcourt Brace & Co., 1959, p. 72.

Union might be preserved if possible. According to Davis's biographer Hudson Strode, the senator from Mississippi — ex-Secretary of War, son of a Revolutionary veteran — "felt coercion and war would be the result [of secession]. The strain brought on an attack of his old bête noire, neuralgia. To his friend, former President Franklin Pierce, Davis declared that 'Civil war has only horror for me.'"[72]

It was taken for granted by the world at large that the president-elect would agree to any plausible compromise to settle the issue. That was the logical construction to be put on such circumstances as, unchecked, would cause untold bloodshed and destruction. What honest leader would desire the rending apart of a nation? Would Lincoln? Surely not. Meetings were held and recommendations made. Yet the president-elect fixed a look of cold indifference on the proposals for conciliation. He was in a way like King George III, who 90 years earlier had brushed away the hope of peace-minded ministers for compromise with the colonies. The king had wanted matters settled on his own terms. So, it seemed, did the incoming president of the United States, who, in truth, had vividly shown his cast of mind in the Cooper Union address, eight months before the election. The address was testy in tone toward the South, lofty and unbending as to the likelihood of reconciliation. Lincoln spoke of his Southern countrymen as "they" — some foreign tribe yapping at the Northern keepers of righteousness.

"Holding as they do," he had said at the Cooper Union in February 1860, "that slavery is morally right, and socially elevating, they cannot cease to demand a full national recognition of it, as a legal right, and a social blessing .... The whole

---

[72] *Ibid.*, pp. 368-369, 387.

atmosphere must be disinfected from all taint of opposition to slavery." It was rhetorical overstatement of a particularly scornful kind. When it came to compromise, "groping for some middle ground between the right and the wrong such as a policy of 'don't care' on a question about which all true men do care" — what kind of policy was that? Did not "true men" — as distinguished presumably from those "false men" on the other side — enjoy the anterior right of final judgment? "[T]hinking it [slavery] wrong, as we do, can we yield to them?" The question answered itself. The righteous deserved to prevail, the unrighteous to fail: possible candidates for Perdition.

There was not much of charity or of hope for sectional conciliation to be hunted up in Candidate Lincoln's New York manifesto. As President-elect Lincoln, he was only giving official effect to the sentiments of the previous winter. No historical cover can hide the fact that Lincoln did not yearn for peace between the rival sections of his nation. To Lyman Trumbull he wrote, on December 10, 1860, "Stand firm. The tug has to come, & better now, than any time hereafter." "The tug"? It was an anodyne way of describing the stakes in his contest with states that were clearly in a mood for secession and, should the necessity arise, war.[73]

Lincoln's correspondence from the post-election period reveals no anxiety on his part concerning the cost of a fratricidal war for the Union. Says Richard Current: Lincoln expected such a war would be short and "quickly won. He did not foresee the long years of bloody conflict. Not so Jefferson Davis, who in his inaugural address as Confederate president predicted that 'the sufferings of millions will bear testimony to the folly and

---

[73] Lincoln, *Speeches and Writings*, Vol. 2, p. 194.

wickedness of our aggressors.'"⁷⁴ Lincoln's miscalculation is one of the costliest in recorded history: similar to the expectation of mutton-chopped Austro-Hungarian emperor in the summer of 1914 that Serbia could be chastised without fuss or bother as revenge for the assassination of the heir to the throne and his wife.

If any one man was responsible for a decision that might bring on war between North and South, that man was Lincoln. He said he gave assurances that the federal government would respect all rights guaranteed under the Constitution.⁷⁵ But in his view these rights were a good deal less prepossessing than even the mildest Southern opinion desired. He had repeatedly scoffed at the notion that the Southern states would secede. Almost contemptuously he dismissed the possibility of secession, just as his party had done before the election. Then, when secession occurred, he mostly ignored it.

The public policy of the Republican party was opposition to slavery extension. This simple statement masked the party's real position — hostility to the entire Southern society in the interest of consolidating Republican power. Lincoln's party had been called the sectional party of division, the dis-union party, the party willing to resort to violence (like the wealthy and influential men who had financed John Brown's raid on Harper's Ferry) in order to dominate the South. Karl Marx called it the faction which, obtaining the federal power, used it to dominate its rivals,

---

⁷⁴ *Ibid.*, p. 90; Current, p. 130; Jefferson Davis, *The Papers of Jefferson Davis*, Vol. 7, Louisiana State University Press, 1992, p. 49.

⁷⁵ To Stephens, a Georgia ex-Whig whom he had known in Congress, and whom he respected, Lincoln wrote that "The South would be in no more danger [concerning slavery] than it was in the days of Washington." Lincoln, *Speeches and Writings*, Vol. 2, p. 190.

economically and politically. The North wanted a controlled source of cheap raw materials and a captive market for it manufactures.

On January 3, 1861, John J. Crittenden, respected senator from Kentucky and ex-Whig, introduced a measure which, with Lincoln's support, could have quieted the feverish nation and prevented the slaughter that was to come. The aged Crittenden — born the week before the signing of the U.S. Constitution — had been pressing for constitutional amendments that would have prohibited slavery in national territory north of the Missouri Compromise line while protecting slavery south of the line. New states were to decide for themselves whether to enter the Union slave or free. The federal government was to be barred from interfering with slavery in states where it already existed, and in the District of Columbia.

Crittenden had been working on these amendments in a special "Committee of 13," created on December 18 to consider all measures relating to the national crisis. Support became widespread. There was never a more astute political observer than ex-President Martin Van Buren, who said the amendments would certainly be ratified by three-fourths of the states. Southern members of the "Committee of 13" let it be known that they might support the Crittenden compromise — if the Republicans would. The Republicans, on Lincoln's counsel — if not under his direction — would not. As a result, the Crittenden compromise remained stalled in the Committee.

That was why Crittenden took the Senate floor on January 3, 1861, to make a dramatic appeal to the country. He proposed that since the committee would not release the measure, it should be submitted to the people in a referendum. If the senators would not enact the Compromise, why not let the people decide? Stephen A. Douglas promptly endorsed the idea. Horace Greeley, famous editor and an influential force in politics, believed a majority of the people favoured Crittenden's plan. The former New York governor Horatio Seymour, a Douglas supporter and advocate of conciliation, said a referendum on the compromise would carry his state by a majority of 150,000. It was no use. Lincoln was of a mind finally to have it out with the South.

In February Virginia's General Assembly called a "peace convention" in Washington, D.C. Twenty-one states sent representatives. Former President John Tyler was chairman. Opinion coalesced around a version of the Crittenden Compromise tailored to maximize free-state support: that is, no new territory would be admitted to the Union without majority consent both from free-state and slave-state senators. The delegates called on Lincoln to solicit his support. The enterprise came to nothing. It was too late.

Crittenden's spirit of moderation would survive amid the holocaust of war. As a member of the House of Representatives in July 1861, he sponsored, along with the future President Andrew Johnson of Tennessee, then a senator, a resolution defining the purpose of the war as restoration of the Union "with all the dignity, equality, and rights of the several states unimpaired." The resolution gained nearly unanimous approval. Crittenden, a Union man through and through, had foreseen and tried to prevent the horrors of war and — though he died before the war's end — the crushing of the defeated South during Reconstruction. His efforts were as noble as they were futile.

All the South ever wanted was "to be left alone." It was not Jefferson Davis and Alexander Stephens who sought war. Both had opposed secession. If Lincoln had not started a war, there would have been no war. His vision of the future discounted the cost of attaining that future. If a war was needed to displace the existing order, war there had to be.

Secretary of State William Seward wanted to pick a fight with a foreign country in order to unite North and South, showing clearly how different from and ignorant of Lincoln's motives Seward was. Lincoln convinced him that foreign intervention must be avoided at all costs. Lincoln, unbeknownst to Seward did not want reconciliation, he wanted supremacy of his party.[76]

It was Lincoln's task now to somehow create support among a populace not of his mind, support necessary for the maintenance and extensions of his party's power.

Peace would not permit it. War was the only way the Republicans could stay alive and prosper.

Lincoln's journey by railroad from Springfield to Washington — he arrived in disguise and by a circuitous route, February 23, having been warned against an assassination attempt — was a generally exuberant party, the gratification of lust for power. By contrast, Jefferson Davis's journey to Montgomery was a solemn passage. Both Davis and the respectful crowds that greeted him along the way were somber, hushed, expectant, dreading — aware of the menace of Lincoln's power. Lincoln was duly inaugurated on March 4. He attempted to assuage Southern fears. "We are not enemies but friends," he said in his inaugural address. "We must not be enemies." He made clear at the same time that there would be no countenancing secession. There was

---

[76] Seward had in mind France and Spain as prospective targets of national indignation. Wary of war, he suggested that stirring up "a threat of danger from abroad would produce a tempest of patriotic ardor that would end all thought of disunion." Van Deusen, p. 242.

no right to leave the Union. Those who stayed would stay on the old terms of apprehension and uncertainty regarding the future exercise of cherished rights.[77]

By using the term "we" Lincoln spoke magisterially as if he was the United States and the deliberate actions of the people of seven states were nothing but a mob of unruly citizens. But the election results showed he did not have solid support even in the North. A minority President might have taken a conciliatory stance in such a case.

---

[77] Lincoln, *Speeches and Writings*, Vol. 2, pp. 215-224.

COUNTRY OR PARTY?

THE AMERICAN "CIVIL WAR" — besides being distinctly un-civil — was not a civil war in the classic sense, a conflict between or among domestic factions. It was a fight between the power of the states and the power of the federal (central) government. It is the great lesson of American history. It is the nucleus of the whole. Just as Holy Week sums up the Bible and Jesus's life, so the War Between the States is the essential picture of America. A nation is its history, and Lincoln stands astride that period — the god who pulled the levers. At no recent date has one man been so singly responsible for war as was Abraham Lincoln for precipitating the War Between the States.

The nation had waited anxiously to learn what Lincoln would say in his inaugural address, the South especially so. The Southern states had seceded because of Lincoln's election. His inaugural address confirmed their fears. He stated that he regarded the Union as still intact, the secession of seven states as a non-fact, a reality not to be countenanced. Lincoln said he would enforce the laws of the Union in all the states, but he softened this declaration by adding that he would use no violence unless it was forced upon him. "The power confided to me will be used to hold, occupy and possess the property and places belonging to the government, and to collect the duties and imposts; but beyond what may be necessary for these objects, there will be no invasion, no using of force against or among the people anywhere." And later on: "In your hands, my dissatisfied fellow countrymen, and not in mine, is the momentous issue of civil war. The government will not assail you. You can have no conflict without being yourself the aggressors."

Most public discussion North and South had up till now spoke of civil war only as an unthinkable horror. Lincoln stated it as a real possibility and indicated that if it came it would be entirely the South's fault.

How is it possible to reconcile the declaration that Lincoln would occupy "the property and places belonging to the government" with the promise that the government would not assail his dissatisfied fellow countrymen who either held or claimed the right to those places? Douglas in the Senate pointed out at once the contradiction: the revenue could not be collected without the ports and an attempt to take the ports would be war. While ostensibly addressing Southerners, Lincoln was really directing those last soothing words to the substantial anti-war elements in the North. His warning that the secessionists would be the aggressors, if civil war occurred, may be significant in light of what he was to be doing exactly a month from that day. (On April 4th Lincoln ordered that a ship be sent to provision Fort Sumter.)

The president said the Union was unbroken. He committed himself to no specific action. He hedged at every point where a specific statement of active policy was expected. Cautious reticence was a lifelong trait of Lincoln, attested to by those who knew him best. Republicans in the House of Representatives discussed coercive measures, but these were dropped. Lincoln was not yet ready for confrontation.

Lincoln was skilled in phrasing his public utterances so as to arouse in each special group just the reaction he desired. Aggressive Republicans fastened on his inaugural pledge to enforce obedience on the secessionist people. To the Northern peace advocates, as well as to the anxious Unionists of the border states, not yet seceded, his words smelled of conciliation. The seven Southern states contemplating the Union from outside understood Lincoln to be issuing threats of coercion. They hastened preparations for defense.

Lincoln was first and foremost a politician. In his personal and public relations, he was always the trimmer. His support had come from widely different sources and for a variety of reasons. The abolitionists voted for him because of the slavery issue. The Northern capitalist interests voted for him because of his favouring the protective tariff, railroad subsidies and national banking. Westerners voted for him because he promised to supply free homesteads and keep Negroes away from them. He had campaigned hard to convince the voters that neither he nor the Republicans would cause the South to secede, and that thus, under the Republicans, things would go on as they had gone before. A sizeable group in the North wanted to settle the differences peacefully. But the more aggressive party men among the Republicans, to whom he was under special obligation, were urging him to use force, even to the waging of war. Conservative sentiment in the North, favouring peace, was a political force to be reckoned with, and stood in opposition to Lincoln's radical supporters who favoured coercion, even war.

Another force pulling Lincoln away from open coercion was the majority in the border slave states that had not seceded but were openly opposed to coercion of the Lower South. The Virginia State Convention, convened on February 13, was still in session, evidently awaiting Lincoln's move. A strongly aggressive policy by Lincoln would satisfy the radical Republicans but would alienate those who favoured peace in the North and precipitate the border states into secession and union with the Confederacy.

It is unclear whether Lincoln thought that the Upper South would secede if he adopted force and thus double the size of the Confederacy. He was told often enough that this was so. Was he willing to take the risk or was he blinded by his own nature? He was a politician and thought in political terms. He offered Cabinet appointments to a few former Whigs from the states not yet seceded and was turned down. Did Lincoln not understand that the South had moved beyond his realm of political manipulation?

What faced him was the threat that enough supporters might defect to weaken his position, divide his party, and destroy the Republicans before they had a chance to establish their power. He had rejected overtures for compromise in December.

At the same time, Lincoln well understood that failure to resolve the crisis at hand would undermine the Republican position. It was apparent that the public was viewing the Republicans, with their hostile attitude toward the South, as the cause of disunity. How could the situation be turned around? The Republicans asked themselves. They answered their own question: induce the Southerners to be regarded as aggressors by the North and the world. By firing first, they would become the villains, taking the Republicans' place as cause of the trouble.

Certainly, the voters knew that the South, which would have remained in the Union had the Democrats won, had seceded because of fear of Republican policies and threats. The Northern majority, even the moderate wing of Lincoln's own party, did not favour a war policy toward the South. If some of these could be made to believe that war was started by the secessionists, they might come over to Lincoln's side. War was obviously the last thing the secessionists wanted, but the matter could be made to appear otherwise.

Unless Lincoln could unite the majority in defense of the authority of his minority government, the two wings of his party — the doves and the hawks, to borrow 20th century terminology — the party would collapse. Both his party and his career would be finished before they could gain momentum. In chastising the Republican killing of the Crittenden Compromise, Stephen Douglas stated the case clearly. Lincoln had a choice between his party and his country.

Between his election victory in November and his inauguration in March Lincoln had seen the popularity of his party decrease. Election losses at the state level in Connecticut, Ohio, and Rhode Island, and a growing nervousness in public sentiment, made this obvious. There was a growing sense that the "Abolitionist Party" was going to make trouble.

The Confederate leaders were not vicious men. Neither were they ignorant, irresponsible, or inexperienced. They were fully aware of the danger of taking the initiative in hostilities. It was obvious then, as it has been obvious since, that peace served their ends far better than it did the North's. How then could they be so blind as to place themselves at this disadvantage?

The Confederate government was moving cautiously, negotiating to avoid hostilities and buy the fort. On February 15, the Confederate Congress requested President Davis to appoint three commissioners to negotiate with the United States on "all questions of disagreement between the two governments." Davis appointed them on February 25. They reached Washington on March 5, the day after Lincoln's inauguration.

Every proposition can be stated positively and negatively. That fact has been known since the Greek masters of rhetoric enunciated it. Lincoln read about it and was intrigued by the concept. Lincoln had studied forensics, debate, rhetoric, oratory with the same zeal that all power seekers give the task. In 1847-8, during his one term in Congress, he was fascinated by the contrast between his own arm-waving, loud, strident declamatory style, and the quiet, reasoned delivery of John C. Calhoun. He determined to copy the Calhoun style. He practiced it, adopted it, and never left it, with the exception of the "lost" Bloomington speech in 1856. His style became quiet. The content remained inflammatory but was veneered with mildness.

In 1848 Lincoln was not nominated by his party for a second term in Congress. Deeply depressed by this rejection, he conferred his law practice on his partner, withdrew to an inner room and for days sat alone, unhappily musing. Slumped in one chair, his legs stretched on another, he meditated on defeat, the uses of power, and the methods of attaining it. After several months he came forth with his own method. Since every proposition can be stated positively or negatively, the way to win in politics is to find an issue, phrase it in a way so that your side of the question is stated in a positive way, forcing your opponent to take the negative. Then you abuse him for being "against" something, rather than "for" it. The exponent of the negative is on the defense immediately.

All the public property that Lincoln had mentioned in his inaugural address had already been taken over peacefully by the seceded states, which had offered to pay for them and assume their share of the government debt. There were two exceptions, as everyone knew. There were still small federal garrison forces at Fort Sumter commanding Charleston Harbor and Fort Pickens at Pensacola.

Two not merely suspicious but actually hostile nations faced each other. Well did Abraham Lincoln know and understand the stakes. It served his purposes that Sumter should fall.

As early as January 19, nine Southern senators in Washington urged avoidance of any act that would afford the provocation for which Republicans in Congress were hoping, so as to involve the Buchanan administration in pre-inauguration hostilities.

The South felt that South Carolina had ceded the land to build Fort Sumter for its own (certainly not New York's or Ohio's!) protection. Suddenly, rather than a protection, Fort Sumter had become a threat. Its guns dominated the harbor. The Confederate States, no longer connected to the government on the Potomac, claimed the right to buy the fort for their own use. For Northerners who opposed secession, ceding the fort would be tantamount to acknowledging the legality of secession.

Major Anderson, commander at Fort Sumter, was allowed by the Southern authorities in Charleston free use of the mails and the purchase of groceries in the local markets. He was not allowed to receive Federal government replacement of men or supplies, as that would be an acknowledgment of U.S. government supremacy.

As things then stood, the only way Lincoln, his administration, and his party could be saved was by an unequivocal assertion of the authority of government, by a mighty exercise of power — that is, by war. By playing out his strategy, he changed our government from federal to consolidated: the most revolutionary and selfish act by one man in our history. This he undertook gladly, indifferent to some of the more unpleasant consequences of his actions.

But Lincoln knew he must not openly make the first aggressive move; that must be done by the secessionists. Fort Sumter presented the best opportunity, but time was short as the garrison was running low on supplies and Anderson was going to withdraw as soon as his larders were empty. Power was slipping away from Lincoln. The only way he could save his power was by using his power — make war. He preferred to save himself rather than his country.

A few days before Buchanan left office, Congress passed the Morrill Tariff Act, which raised duties far higher than rates established by the Confederate Congress. This gave anxiety to Northern manufacturers and exporters, and to the administration as the lower rates would deflect imports (and exports) to the South, weakening the prosperity of Northern business and reducing Federal government custom revenues. The tariff differential would also invite further states to join the Confederacy. The *New York Times* and many other Republican papers was alarmed at the tariff differential. The Northern economy could not afford a free trade empire in North America. The Confederacy offered free use of the Mississippi and its port of New Orleans to the U.S., but the press was full of claims that Northern trade would be blocked.

That Lincoln wanted to take aggressive actions, that his hostile attitude toward the South had caused Southern secession, was plain to see. As time progressed, the only opposing force that could stop him — Congress — weakened with the resignations of Southern Democratic senators and congressmen. Republican proportions in that body expanded greatly.

Because the Confederates fired the first shot, the North and Lincoln were quick to blame the war on them. That view still predominates among historians and, of course, casual observers of the historical record. If the conflict had not been lighted by the Fort Sumter crisis, it would have been lit from some other spark, because Lincoln wanted it lit; but he wanted to make the South seem to strike the match. He knew how simply events are seen from a distance. Fantasy is simple. It fits together, without thought of a price. Truth is more complex, more difficult. Fantasy is easier to understand and easier to sell.

The firing of the "first shot" was not the first hostile act; the South was not the aggressor. Southerners wanted only to get out of the Union as quietly and quickly as possible. Firing on Fort Sumter put the Southerners at a great moral and material disadvantage. It gave Lincoln what he wanted: an excuse to invade; and it provided a casus belli where there previously there had not been one sufficient to excite many Northerners, apart from abolitionists and Republican party zealots.

At Fort Sumter Lincoln was able — in Hegelian terms — to take thesis and force the South into antithesis. By his own admission he maneuvered to make the South appear the villain. The leader of the party of "disunion" became the standard bearer of Union. What he meant, in fact, by "the Union" was a thing of his own invention.

The War Between the States was the greatest tragedy in American history. It destroyed $13 billions of property. It killed at least 763,000 soldiers, probably more.[78] It ruined the health of a good part of the surviving Southerners, soldier and civilian alike. Estimates of the deaths of civilians, including slaves, from the brutal invasion of the South are in the hundreds of thousands and are steadily rising as more is known.

The destruction wrought by the 1861-65 war is expressible not only in lives and property but in principle. The war destroyed the limited government created by the founding fathers and made possible a revolution replacing the old government, based as it was on limitations of power, with a new structure formed from consolidated power.

---

[78] "New Estimate Raises Civil War Death Toll," *The New York Times*, April 2, 2012.

THE TRAP IS SPRUNG

THE DEVELOPMENT OF THE FORT SUMTER crisis is so complex that relatively few people understand it. Events do make it clear that the South feared war and took every step to avoid it. Major Anderson did not want to cause a civil war. President Buchanan considered it not in his power to make war on the Southern states that had seceded between December 20, 1860, and February 1, 1861 (South Carolina, Mississippi, Florida, Alabama, Georgia, Louisiana, and Texas). Even Seward, Lincoln's Secretary of State, seemed to consider that prospect unthinkable. Most people looked upon the thought of war between the North and South with horror and dread.

The specific precipitating force, as every schoolchild soon enough learns, was the Southern bombardment of Fort Sumter at 4:30 a.m. on April 12, 1861. Little things proverbially lead to large ones. The attack on Sumter, the war's only sizable military engagement in which no one died, magnified the premises on which the two sides took their stands. A Northern fort on Confederate territory was, from the Southern viewpoint, a contradiction of sovereignty. From the Northern viewpoint, a Southern attack on a federal installation, wherever located, was an act of war.

Navy Captain Gustavus Vasa Fox had recommended to Lincoln on March 13 that a combined naval and military expedition be sent to Charleston. The Cabinet, excepting Postmaster General Montgomery Blair and the often-equivocal Salmon P. Chase, Secretary of the Treasury, had voted against such a course. For which there were essentially three reasons. Some feared such an expedition might fail. Others thought the move would stamp The

U.S. government as the aggressor, while a third group thought it wrong to initiate warfare over such an issue.

So, Lincoln sent Fox to Charleston to investigate. Fox arrived there on March 21 and went out to Sumter the same evening. He and Major Anderson agreed that the garrison would be out of supplies and thus have to vacate by April 15. Anderson did not like the idea of a military expedition. Fox returned to Washington, still enthusiastic for his plan. Through most of the crisis Anderson remained without official orders and had no more idea than anyone else in the country what Lincoln planned.

On the very day Fox arrived in Charleston, Lincoln sent there his close friend and political intimate Ward H. Lamon, a native of Virginia and his former law partner in Illinois. His decision to send Lamon on the heels of Fox makes for interesting surmises. What Lincoln told Lamon is unknown. Lamon himself in his recollections merely says he was sent out "on a confidential mission"; he implies that one aim was to determine the extent of Unionist feeling in South Carolina. He arrived in Charleston on Saturday, March 23, and on Sunday visited James L. Petigru, heretofore a notable Unionist. Petigru told Lamon that there was no longer any Unionist sentiment to be found in the State. Lincoln would have to leave South Carolina to peaceful secession or else go to war.

On Monday, Governor Francis W. Pickens told Lamon that South Carolina, having ceded Fort Sumter to the Federal government for protection of the harbor, found that duty now to rest with South Carolina and the Confederacy. The South could not permit Northern domination and potential threat to a major port.

Lincoln's reinforcement of Sumter would be an act of war. Lamon made both Pickens and Anderson believe that the garrison at Fort Sumter would soon be withdrawn and that his trip was merely to prepare the way for that event. Whether this was innocent (in that Lincoln had not revealed his intention) or guileful is unknown. Lamon left Charleston on the night of the 25th, arrived in Washington on the 27th and reported to Lincoln.[79] What was Lincoln's purpose in sending Lamon to Charleston? Certainly not to prepare the way for evacuation as Lamon made Governor Pickens and Major Anderson think. It was to learn the Southern feeling about reinforcing Fort Sumter. Lamon may not himself have divined the real reason from the calculating Lincoln. But Lincoln did now know — Lamon had it directly — that, reinforcing the fort would cause the South to attack Fort Sumter. It was precisely the opportunity he wanted.

Lamon promised Pickens that Fort Sumter would be ceded back to South Carolina. On April 1, Lincoln sent word, through Seward to John A. Campbell — an Alabamian and U.S. Supreme Court justice — that Lamon had no authority to make such a promise. He had Seward state, "Lamon did not go to Charleston under any commission or authority from Mr. Lincoln."[80] However, Lamon himself recounts the conversation between Lincoln, Seward and himself when Lincoln asked him to go. Who was lying, the openhearted Lamon, or the calculating Lincoln?

---

[79] Lamon, *Recollections of Abraham Lincoln*, pp. 68-79.

[80] Henry Connor, *John Archibald Campbell, Associate Justice of the United States, 1853-1861*, Houghton Mifflin Co., 1920, p. 127.

According to Secretary of the Navy Gideon Welles, Lincoln, at some point in late March, informed his cabinet that he would reinforce Sumter. On March 29 (two days after Lamon's return) Lincoln took the opinions of each cabinet member on the relief of Fort Sumter. This time there was a marked change from the opinion given two weeks earlier. Now only Seward and Caleb Smith wanted to evacuate, on grounds that it was necessary to do so to avoid war, and desirable to avoid war. The others now wanted to reinforce Sumter. What had changed their opinion? Lincoln's determination, firmly held, or Lincoln's and the cabinet's knowledge that reinforcing the fort would indeed cause war, and war was what they wanted?

This decision, so horrible in its effects, was a gem-like example of Lincoln's political creed: namely, that to win in politics, you create a situation in which your opponent can be made the villain, the partisan of evil, a man of the dark side. It was Lincoln's political skills that made possible this Manichean framework. It was Lincoln's failure as a man that made him willing to do it. He destroyed his government, his nation, and the lives of his countrymen. The phoenix that rose from the ashes of 1865 was a different government, a different nation.

On the same day, March 29, Lincoln directed the Secretaries of War and the Navy to prepare a force to move by sea as early as April 6. The destination was not stated in the order, making the aggressive intent less obvious, but the government had Charleston in mind. Secrecy governed the preparations for the move on Sumter and on Fort Pickens in Florida. Even the two cabinet secretaries, charged as they were with overseeing the preparations, were to know nothing of what was afoot and afloat.

In the first days of April came the upsetting news of Republican electoral reverses in Ohio, Connecticut, and Rhode Island. The support that had put the Republicans in power was fast ebbing away. Lincoln's friends said he never read a book through, merely extracting what he needed for his practical political purposes. A man who liked to read would not have had the inclinations or the time to spend in the endless political maneuvering which occupied Lincoln's adult life. But now he was putting into use skills honed in 30 years of law practice and unceasing political striving.

He met a group of seven or nine Republican governors — the precise number is unknown — in a mysterious conference from April 3-6. All were members of the pro-aggression faction. It is thought that they and Lincoln met to pledge combined action and support in case the Confederates should show fight.

After meeting with the governors, Lincoln, on April 4, conferred with Col. John B. Baldwin, a leader of the Unionists in the Virginia convention — this at the request of Seward. Throughout this period Seward seemed to be making continual efforts to preserve the peace. Not so Lincoln. Baldwin went with an associate to see Seward, who sent the pair to Lincoln. Lincoln took Baldwin alone into a bed chamber and locked the door. Baldwin, after the war, recounted the episode to Robert Lewis Dabney, a prominent Presbyterian theologian and minister, Baldwin sought earnestly to convince Lincoln to stay his hand so as to keep Virginia in the Union and with her the other border states. "Colonel Baldwin assured him solemnly that the Republicans fatally misunderstood the South .... Lincoln's native good sense, with Colonel Baldwin's evident sincerity, seemed not to open his eyes to this truth ... he frowned and contorted his features, exclaiming, 'I ought to have known this sooner! You are too late, sir, too late!' ... Colonel Baldwin understood this as a clear intimation that the policy of coercion was determined on, and within the last four days."

Baldwin suggested a Lincolnian pledge of non-interference "with the Constitution and laws, and the rights of the States."

Lincoln, according to Dabney's account, appeared to see conciliation as undermining the Republican high tariff policy. Nothing came of the interview, for which Dabney blamed "factious counselors, blinded by hatred and contempt of the South." Dabney saw the radical governors Lincoln had spoken with as full of zeal for "a strong and centralised government" — such a government as the South would not stand for. And that was that.[81] To Baldwin and others Lincoln stated that he could not allow secession because he would lose "my revenue."

During the afternoon of April 4 Lincoln also saw Captain Fox, who was to have charge of the Fort Sumter expedition, and told him of his final determination to send relief to Major Anderson. He said Governor Francis W. Pickens of South Carolina would be notified before the expedition could reach Charleston. That same day Lincoln drafted a letter to Anderson, copied and signed by the Secretary of War, informing him that relief would be sent him.

A notice to Governor Pickens, written in Lincoln's own hand, was dated April 6. He took pains to write it himself. The message he gave to R.S. Chew, an official of the State Department, with a letter of instruction telling Chew to read the statement to the Governor and give him a copy of it, if Fort Sumter had not been evacuated or attacked. If the Fort had been evacuated or attacked

---

[81] "Interview Between President Lincoln and Col. John B. Baldwin, April 4, 1861, Statement and Evidence," Staunton, Va., Spectator Job Office, 1866; R. L. Dabney, D.D., "Memoir of a Narrative Received of Colonel John B. Baldwin, of Staunton, Touching the Origin of the War," *Southern Historical Society Papers*, Vol. 1, Number 6, 1876, pp. 443-454.

he was to seek no interview but was to return immediately. The message to Governor Pickens was in these words:

"I am directed by the President of the United States to notify you to expect an attempt will be made to supply Fort Sumter with provisions only; and that, if such an attempt be not resisted, no effort to throw in men, arms, or ammunition will be made without further notice, or in case of an attack upon the Fort."[82]

Lincoln was a rare master of the written word. He had the lawyer's skill of so phrasing a sentence so that it conveyed precisely the meaning he wished it to convey. He could do more than that: he could make the same sentence say one thing to one person and something entirely different to another, and in each case carry the different meaning he intended. To the apprehensive Confederates the message was a direct challenge: I am going to hold this fort and control your harbor. This was directly opposite to the impression he had given the Confederates all along and was a threat that force would be used if provisioning was not allowed. To the Northern reader of the message the words meant only that the government was merely feeding hungry soldiers. Northern men would see no threats, they would infer that their government sought to avoid force. It is not possible that Lincoln's known perspicacity could be blind to the different interpretations his subtle words would shape.

The message was not only skillfully phrased, it was most carefully timed. It was read to Governor Pickens in the presence of General Beauregard on the evening of April 8. News that a large expedition was being readied to sail had been in the newspapers for a week. Not until April 8 had Charleston been

---

[82] Samuel Wylie Crawford, *The Genesis of the Civil War: The Story of Sumter, 1860-61*, Hardpress Publishing, 2012, p. 404.

suspected as its destination. The press did not know until April 9 that Governor Pickens had been notified. Utmost secrecy was maintained about the two expeditions so that the Confederates thought the whole force was to be concentrated at Charleston, not realizing that part was going to Florida. To the Confederates a formidable aggression was advancing.

The tables were now turned on the Southerners. Lincoln was well out of his dilemma; at least he had had time for deliberation. The South had had the tactical advantage of being able to wait until Anderson had to evacuate. Now two evils had presented themselves. A quick choice was required. The Confederacy had either to take the fort before help could arrive, accepting any reproach for initiating the conflict, or stand by quietly and see the fort provisioned. To allow the provisioning mean t not only an indefinite postponement to Confederate possession of the fort, but also the consequences of seeming to retreat before the threat of force. Nor could the Confederates be sure that, allowing "provisions only," they would not see — contrary to Lincoln's assurance — men, arms, and ammunition arriving at the fort. Not only would a Union-held fort symbolize the incompleteness of their existence as a separate nation — it would continue, as it always had done, to dominate the port and the city. Lincoln's astute strategy had thrust the South into this dilemma.

Events now hurried to their inevitable climax. Lincoln's correspondence and that of his fellows indicates that he did not expect the South to retreat. As soon as General Beauregard heard Lincoln's statement — or, better said, ultimatum — he telegraphed the news to the Confederate Secretary of War, L.P. Walker. Walker at once ordered that the Sumter garrison be isolated: its mail stopped, and purchase of local stores and provisions forbidden. On this same day the Confederate commissioners at Washington had received a copy of a memorandum filed in the State Department by Seward, dated March 15, in which the Secretary declined any official intercourse with them.

The commissioners telegraphed that news to their government. Realising they had been deceived and knowing that their mission had failed, they prepared to leave Washington. Thus, on April 8, Jefferson Davis learned of two separate, ominous-seeming actions by the federal government. On the following day Beauregard seized the mails as they came from Fort Sumter and discovered a letter from Anderson to the War Department, disclosing that he already knew of Fox's coming and indicating that the Northern fleet intended to force its way into the harbor. On the tenth came the news that the fleet had sailed from New York. Walker then directed Beauregard to demand the evacuation of Fort Sumter and, if refused, to "reduce it." The South had waited two full days after receiving word of Lincoln's message before deciding what to do. Robert Toombs, Confederate Secretary of State, objected to attacking the Fort. "It is unnecessary; it puts us in the wrong; it is fatal,"[83] he said. The Confederates, however, believed that Lincoln had already taken the offensive. They regarded the problem as now no longer political but military. To them it was a simple question of whether they should take the fort before the fleet arrived, or wait and have to fight both fort and fleet.

On April 11 Beauregard demanded that Anderson evacuate Sumter, with a guarantee that his troops would be allowed to leave in honour. Anderson rejected the demand but told the officer sent to him that he would be starved out in a few days anyway. Beauregard reported this remark to Walker. Walker

---

[83] Michael Burlingame, *Lincoln: A Life*, Vol. 2, Johns Hopkins University, 2008, p. 128.

told him that they did not want to bombard Fort Sumter and that if Major Anderson would state when he would evacuate, Beauregard should "avoid the effusion of blood." The Confederate officials thought there was a chance to get the fort without the showdown to be caused by the fleet. But Lincoln had timed his message carefully with the movement of Fox. Inciting attack was his aim, and that of his party. On the same day Beauregard received word that the *Harriet Lane*, one of Fox's ships, had been sighted off the harbor. It was expected that the whole fleet would arrive by next day. Nevertheless, further Confederate efforts were made to avoid a fight. Beauregard sent a second message to Anderson, telling him that he would not fire if Anderson would evacuate. To this Anderson replied that he would evacuate by April 15th unless before that date he received supplies or orders from the government. As supplies were to be on hand the next day, the answer was not satisfactory. Anderson would be supplied and would not evacuate. Anderson was notified at 3:20 a.m. on the 12th that bombardment would commence in one hour's time.

At 4:30 a.m., bombardment of Fort Sumter began. On the afternoon of the following day Anderson surrendered. The three vessels of the fleet which lay outside were unable to get into the harbor because of high seas and failure of the rest of the fleet to arrive. There were no casualties during the bombardment, but the mere news that the attack on the fort had begun ignited in the North a roaring flame of anger. The "rebels" had fired the first shot; they had chosen to begin war.

Lincoln's strategy was a brilliant success. A wavering support, spreading discontent with his policies, growing newspaper criticism, defections in his political strength, electoral defeats — all were swept away when the word went out: The South had fired on the flag. Lincoln seized the ripe moment, called out the militia, and committed his administration to war. The border states did not see his action in so admirable a light. Four of them — North Carolina, Virginia, Tennessee, and Arkansas — seceded. Kentucky, Missouri, Delaware, and Maryland, slave states all, might disapprove of continued membership in the Union, but their power was as nothing against that of the national government.

Lincoln had lived up completely to the character ascribed to him by the seceding states. They seceded because they said he was hostile to them and they were not safe under him. His public words denied it; his private words and his actions confirmed it.

Lincoln had planned war all along. Such a course was certainly compatible with his position in the Republican Party and his place in the political spectrum. There is good reason to believe that Lincoln had decided that there was no other way than war for the salvation of his career, his administration, and his party. It is foolish to justify his actions and their results on grounds of saving the Union. Lincoln did not save the Union; he destroyed it and built a new one.

Having decided on war, he understood that his next step was to maneuver his opponents into firing the first shot, so that they might be branded as the aggressors, and take the blame. Captain Fox remarked afterward that it seemed very important to Lincoln that South Carolina "should stand before the civilized world as having fired upon bread."[84]

Nothing could justify the hypocrisy of Lincoln's actions or — infinitely worse — the damage he did to the lives of his people and the spirit of his nation. But justifying it we have, besides

---

[84] Bruce Catton, *The Coming Fury*, Doubleday, 1961, p. 297.

praising, lauding, and sanctifying it. There is deep irony in this familiar posture of Lincoln-worship.

That he started the war brands Lincoln forever as a failure as a statesman. That he transferred the blame to his opponents labels him as a successful politician: not so much an accolade, perhaps, as an accusation under the circumstances of his service. Lincoln never admitted that he had maneuvered the country into war. To have done so would have been to tarnish his accomplishment by bringing the blame back to himself. No written word of his contains that confession. There are very few written words of his that are other than political. Candor was not his goal in writing.

Beside the facts of the opening of the war, what else points to Lincoln's stratagems? Two statements by him to Captain Fox are suggestive. Fox relates that in their conference of April 4 the President told him that he had decided to let the expedition go and that a messenger would be sent to the authorities at Charleston before Fox could possibly get there. Captain Fox reminded Lincoln of the short time he gave him to organize the expedition and reach the desired point. Lincoln replied, "You will best fulfill your duty to your country by making the attempt." On May 1, Lincoln wrote to Fox, who had been chagrined that his fleet had not reached Sumter before it fell. In his letter Lincoln said, "You and I both anticipated that the cause of the country would be advanced by making the attempt to provision Fort Sumter, even if it should fail, and it is no small consolation now to feel that our anticipations are justified by the result."[85] Didn't this convey that the real objective of the expedition was accomplished? Relieving Fort Sumter was not the objective; starting a war while shifting the blame for it was the real aim.

---

[85] Lincoln, *Speeches and Writings*, Vol. 2, pp. 237-38.

Lincoln's two secretaries, John G. Nicolay and John Hay were Lincoln partisans. They came close to divulging their patron's strategy, almost quoting Lincoln's general philosophy of politics when they say, referring to Sumter: "Abstractly it was enough that the Government was in the right. But to make the issue safe he determined that in addition the rebellion should be put in the wrong." Later they say, "President Lincoln in deciding the Sumter question, had adopted a simple but effective policy. To use his own words, he determined to send bread to Anderson: if the rebels fired on that, they would not be able to convince the world that he had begun the civil War."

The phrase "send bread" was characteristic Lincoln cant. He wasn't "sending bread." Anderson had been getting fresh food every day in the Charleston markets. Simple words, slogans, metaphors, demagoguery were the president's own produce. Nicolay and Hay said, "When he finally gave the order that the fleet should sail he was master of the situation; master if the rebels hesitated or repented, because they would thereby forfeit their prestige with the South; master if they persisted, for he would then command a united North"[86]

Before the expedition reached Charleston, his political opponents in the North expressed suspicion of a design to force civil war upon the country in order to save the Republican Party from the disasters threatened in the recent elections, and to strengthen America's first purely sectional party, only recently risen on a fragile base. After fighting began he was roundly accused of having deliberately provoked war by mounting a demonstration against Charleston in sailing a naval force into its harbor. For a good period, the essential Republicans had been

---

[86] Nicolay and Hay, Vol. 3, pp. 38, 44, 62.

demanding action to save the party. As soon as news of preparation of the fleet appeared, Republican papers began to assert that if war came the rebels would be the aggressors.[87] For the Democrats in Congress, more outnumbered by the Republicans with each Southern resignation, opposition was futile. No power in Congress was available to oppose him.

When the news came of the bombardment at Charleston, the Providence, Rhode Island, *Daily Post* published an editorial entitled "WHY?" "We are to have civil war, if at all, because Abraham Lincoln loves a party better than he loves his Country." After commenting on what seemed to be a sudden change of policy with respect to Sumter, the paper continued: "Why? We think the reader will perceive why. Mr. Lincoln saw an opportunity to inaugurate civil war without appearing in the character of an aggressor. There are men in Fort Sumter, he said, who are nearly out of provisions. They ought to be fed. We will attempt to feed them. Certainly, nobody can blame us for that. The secessionists, who are both mad and foolish, will resist us. They will commence civil war. Then I will appeal to the North to aid me in putting down rebellion, and the North must respond. How can it do otherwise? And sure enough, how can we do otherwise?"

Congressman Alexander Long, Democrat of Ohio, said in a speech before the House on April 8, 1864, that when Lincoln heard the news that the Confederates had fired on Fort Sumter, he exclaimed, exultantly, "I knew they would do it!" The Republicans attempted unsuccessfully to expel Congressman

---

[87] Columbus, Ohio, *Crisis*, April 4, 1861; *The New York Times*, April 8, 10, 1861; *The Baltimore Sun*, April 10, 1861.

Long from the House on the grounds that he was a sympathizer with the rebellion.[88]

To Lincoln's critics, as to many others, the Sumter strategy might seem transparent. Yet it worked. History could deal with the details. Lincoln had for now the initiative. Even the Douglas Democrats found it necessary to rally 'round the flag. When the only choice was between Northern prosperity and their Southern fellow citizens there was no doubt where they would be. Stephen Douglas himself called at the White House to declare his solidarity with the man who had defeated him for the nation's leadership. War had begun. A different kind of history was being made.

---

[88] *Congressional Globe*, 38 Cong. 1 Session, p. 1499 et seq.

Epilogue:
"Enslaving Free Men"

THE MORAL GRANDEUR of Abraham Lincoln, as I noted at the beginning of this study, has become an article of faith for a large majority of Americans. What we need to bear in mind is that moral grandeur is usually accomplished at someone else's expense.

The bill that Lincoln presented to American history is a costly and intimidating one: a war won, a social revolution effected, at catastrophic cost to the American people. The phrase "the American people" is deliberately chosen. This is because the obvious victims of the war were Southerners: multiple generations of them, killed or ruined economically by the North's war of conquest. Wars have a certain impartiality, nonetheless: They affect, in every way possible, everyone involved. Even the victors pay a price. The North, which enlisted more men than did the South, having more men to enlist in the first place, lost more men than the South.

The reunited nation sustained losses of another kind as a triumphant federal government shifted its constitutional premises, redefining the very meaning of America. To many Northerners at the time this was well and good. Many still see it thus. They reckon today, even so, with the price tag of the new premises — larger than was suspected as recently as half a century ago.

The cost of Mr. Lincoln's War was largest, of course, in terms of human life. We have noticed already the new estimate of the death toll on both sides — a combined 752,000, against the traditional rough count of 618,222. The demographic historian David Hacker, of Binghamton University, using newly digitized census figures from 1850 to 1880, recently determined that earlier estimates by amateur historians had been too low. At that, the war was almost unimaginably bloody, with one in 10 men of military age dying from shot, shell, or disease.[89] A comparable loss — 2.5 percent to the present American population of about 300 million would amount to 7.5 million deaths — a truly unthinkable number, at least to Americans.

Indeed, the total of deaths at Shiloh — 23,000 — equaled the total for all America's wars to that point: The Revolution, the War of 1812, the Mexican War. Military hospitals were grisly places, where surgeons doubled as butchers. Says the historian Paul Johnson: "More arms and legs were chopped off in the Civil War than in any other conflict in which America has been engaged." Walt Whitman, too old for military service, assisted with a certain nobility of spirit in military hospitals. He "considered the volume and intensity of the suffering totally, disproportionate to any objective gained by the war."[90]

The economic disaster that befell the South was no less pronounced. The South lost its social order along with incalculable physical and economic resources — buildings, homes, bridges, factories, railroads, ports. Gen. William Tecumseh Sherman, famous for the acknowledgement that "War is hell," cut a 60-mile-wide swath of destruction as he marched. ("And so we sang the chorus from Atlanta to the sea/While we were marching through Georgia.") Of Columbia, S.C., following

---

[89] "New Estimate Raises Civil War Death Toll," *The New York Times*, April 2, 2012.

[90] Paul Johnson, *A History of the American People*, HarperCollins, 1998, pp. 488-489.

Sherman's visit, a Northern reporter wrote: "It is now a wilderness of ruins. Its heart is but a mass of blackened chimneys and crumbling walls. Two thirds of the buildings in the place were burned, including, without exception, everything in the business portion. Not a store, office, or shop escaped." It all had to be rebuilt — or replaced, at immense labor and cost. The South's share of national wealth fell from 30 percent in 1860 to 12 percent in 1870.[91]

The blow to the South's ability to support itself, far less prosper, had been staggering, guaranteeing poverty for most, black and white. The Reconstruction activities of Northern troops, carpetbaggers, and scalawags made possible such advances as the provision of public schools but in the process embittered the South, whose residents recognized themselves as not just a defeated but also a captive people — press-ganged back into a union they had hoped to abandon. The experience poisoned Northern and Southern relationships for decades. It became a Southern commonplace that "damyankee" was a single word.

Not for decades — indeed, not until after the Second World War — would the South regain anything like its old prosperity. As late as 1938, President Franklin D. Roosevelt called the South "the nation's Economic Problem number one." His predecessor, the 16th president, had not reckoned with such an outcome when he put his foot down regarding conciliation of the Southerners who had given him not one vote in 1860. The oddity of Lincoln's situation lay in the division the election — never mind the attack on Fort Sumter — had signaled in the electorate. How is it possible even to contemplate dealing with such a situation by fire

---

[91] Sidney Andrews, *The South Since the War*, Louisiana State University Press, 2004, p. 33; James McPherson, *Abraham Lincoln and the Second American Revolution*, Oxford University Press, 1990., p. 12.

and sword? The unreality of Lincoln's position as aggressor-conciliator is among the many points that escape his modern apologists.

Lincoln had vetted with his advisors the objective of limited war: the defeat of insurrection, the re-incorporation of the South into the Union. The matter had gotten out of hand. The war of 1861-65 was no limited war. It was *guerre a outrance*, as the French say; war to the utmost. There is seemingly a human capacity for underestimating the stakes whenever war looms. The German general staff in 1914 had planned on an early triumph over the French, capped by negotiation of peace on, naturally, German terms. The reality of the machine gun reduced the fantasy of the planners to stagnation in the mud of the Western front. If Lincoln, as Garry Wills notes, was "the least romantic man where war was concerned," did he not understand, with the cavalry fighter Nathan Bedford Forrest, that "War means fighting, and fighting means killing"?[92]

Say the casualties of war had been a "mere" 250,000 — a third of Dr. David Hacker's estimate. Was that not an immense toll, in and of itself, to exact of one's countrymen? That they were countrymen, sentenced by the president of their once-united nation to mow each other down without pity or regret, is the disturbing piece of business here. Call the war a "civil war," call it a war between states formerly conjoined; the victims (including fresh immigrants from Ireland and Germany) were Americans: "brother fightin' brother and killin' one another," as a pop song from the 1961-65 Centennial put the matter with stark realism.

Lincoln had let it happen. Actually, it was more than that: He had invited the killing: his theory of Union against the South's

---

[92] Garry Wills, *Lincoln at Gettysburg: The Words that Remade America*, Simon and Schuster, 1990, p. 77.

divergent theory. The United States, as Lincoln saw it, was an experiment. Successful secession — McPherson makes this point — "would destroy the experiment." The dis-united states would become "a dozen pitiful, squabbling countries, the laughingstock of the world" and "enshrine the idea of inequality."

Chattel slavery was an expression of that idea but hardly the only one on view. At the time of the national founding, only a minority of white men could vote, and no white women at all, far less slaves of either sex. Equality had not been an idea that intrigued the founding generation. To Patrick Henry the essentials of free government had been "justice, moderation, temperance, frugality, and virtue." The Declaration of Independence had proclaimed, a little ambiguously, that "all men are created equal." Yet the Constitutional Convention, a mere 11 years later, had left the slavery to the states for the sake of national unity. The importation of slaves, by constitutional provision, was to be abolished in 20 years but not the institution itself. Moreover, three-fifths of the nation's slaves were to be counted in the apportionment of both representatives and direct taxes among the states.

Lincoln, an opponent of slavery, enterprisingly defined national intentions to suit himself. At Gettysburg, he summoned the nation to "a new birth of freedom." At the start of 1863, by proclamation, he had freed the slaves, meaning those slaves, a small minority, under Union military jurisdiction. A tragic but at the same time endlessly complex problem was succumbing to force.

The matter of the South's four million slaves drives most discussions of the war and its cost. Yes, of course the war was essential, the conventional defense of Lincoln goes. What should he have done — condemn the slaves to endless servitude? Two larger questions demand treatment:

Did the problem require solution at precisely that moment — in 1860?

Did the problem require solution at such cost?

That slavery as an institution was doomed is clear enough today and doomed in the short run rather than the long. History, along with moral witness, had turned against it. By 1860 "the peculiar institution" was extinct everywhere in the Western world save the Southern states, Cuba, and Brazil. The opulence of some planters fed the assumption that slavery was essential to Southern prosperity. In fact, as the economist Thomas J. DiLorenzo has noted, "[S]lave labor is inherently inefficient compared to free labor. Slaves have very few, if any, incentives to work productively, to acquire new skills, and to improve their productivity levels, since they do not stand to benefit from doing so. Furthermore, capital-intensive agriculture and industry began to render labor-intensive production, including slave labor, uncompetitive."[93]

On what basis might one have expected slavery to continue indefinitely if the economic basis said to justify it was faulty? In due course (unless the Lincoln legend cancels all lessons of logic) the South voluntarily, in some manner or another, would have rid itself of slavery. All the more quickly might the South have acted save — ironically — for the abolitionist movement. Abolitionists hit out at the South with insults and abuse, driving Southerners to determined defenses of an institution that Southerners were as morally equipped as Northerners to see rationally if allowed time for reflection.

Question No. 2 stands in proximity to this one because the counting of cost is the most rational of activities whenever great steps are contemplated. That the abolition of slavery in 1863 was

---

[93] Thomas J. DiLorenzo, *The Real Lincoln*, p. 47.

a higher end than the preservation of 752,000 lives and the prevention of economic ruin in half the nation is the point Lincoln apologists seem unwilling to engage. It deserves mention that American deaths in World War II — 416,000 — were less than three-fifths of all Union and Confederate deaths. The 1861-65 war's estimated death toll of 752,000 represented 2.5 percent of all Americans then alive. Alone, the saving of innocent life has always been deemed a cardinal moral principle. It was nevertheless not a principle that engaged the 16th president's interest as Union warships, in April 1861, made for Charleston Harbor.

Curiouser and curiouser — as Alice said, in the classic novel published by "Lewis Carroll," in the year of Appomattox — became Lincoln's efforts to justify the destruction he had set in train by refusing compromise with the South. Speaking at Gettysburg, near the end of 1863, he threw atop the first corpses to be buried there a political rationale for their deaths. Four score and seven years ago, he announced, our fathers had "brought forth on this continent a new nation" — one "dedicated to the proposition that all men are created equal." They had? It depended on whether you saw the Declaration or the Constitution as the founding document. Lincoln had the right to prefer the former, but his choice turned U.S. history inside out, imposing victor's terms on the losers, who, but for lack of military success, would have had much more to say on the matter.

Equality, whatever so broad a term might actually mean, became the national touchstone: argued over with passion in 21st century disputes over medical care and income distribution. The national government, in Washington, D.C., necessarily (given Lincoln's logic) took over from the states the direction of affairs. The idea of states and local communities as the basic social units, closest to the people, and most knowledgeable as to their needs, could never fade out entirely. The 10th amendment to the

Constitution reserved to the states and the people those rights not vouchsafed to Washington; the trouble was that the rights Washington would claim as its own expanded dramatically following the war. The balance of power shifted.

James McPherson writes: "Eleven of the first twelve amendments of the Constitution limited the powers of the national government; six of the next seven dramatically expanded those powers at the expense of states and individuals. In place of the 'thou shalt nots' of ten of the first eleven amendments, the six post-war amendments included the phrase 'Congress shall have the power to enforce this article." Sen. Lot M. Morrill of Maine understood well enough what was afoot. Debating the 14th amendment, with its definition of U.S. citizenship and subsequent guarantee of privileges and immunities to all citizens, Morrill said: "No nation hitherto has cherished a liberty so universal …. [This] civil and political revolution has changed the fundamental principles of our Government."[94]

The historian and Civil War chronicler Shelby Foote more than a century later would put his finger on a crucial, and profoundly illustrative, detail: "Before the war it was always the United States 'are.' After the war, it was the United States 'is.' It made us an 'is.'"[95] Not always to our detriment; frequently to our benefit. So, it had been, nevertheless, with the opposite arrangement — the spacious liberty, the sensitive leadership that flowed from the founders' reckoning that local folk generally knew better than anyone else what they needed, and also how to obtain it.

Matters could have been worse. The old abolitionist congressman Thaddeus Stevens, grim as death, had wanted to "treat this [war] as a radical revolution, and free every slave —

---

[94] McPherson, pp. 138, 142.
[95] http://www.pbs.org/kenburns/civil-war/

slay every traitor — burn every rebel mansion, if those things be necessary to preserve" the nation. Wendell Phillips, the orator and reformer, known as the "Golden Trumpet of Abolition," depicted the war as "primarily a social revolution." Phillips had advocated taking to pieces "the whole social structure of the Gulf States." The temper of the French Revolution showed itself now and again in the pronouncements of the American radicals.

At that, the revolution wrought by Lincoln was damaging enough to American ideals that bore only small relationship to the purposes originally at hand — the suppression of Southern desire to be done with a union increasingly unfriendly to their way of doing business.

"I'm not sure anybody won the war," declared Shelby Foote. "It's a tragedy. On the face of it, the North won the war. But the bill for winning it was huge in human values, not to mention human lives."[96]

In the tragedy that Foote remarked and millions enacted, the central character was the towering, white-marbled figure we know as Lincoln; Father Abraham; the Great Emancipator. It is a pretty story. Like many a pretty story, it crumbles at the touch.

---

[96] *Ibid.*

SELECT BIBLIOGRAPHY

Andrews, Sidney. *The South Since the War*. Louisiana State University Press, 2004.

Beveridge, Albert J. *Abraham Lincoln: A Life*. Houghton Mifflin Company, 1928.

Boucher, Chauncey S. *The Nullification Controversy in South Carolina*. University of North Chicago, 1916.

Bradford, M.E. *The Reactionary Imperative: Essays Literary and Political*. Sherwood Sugden, 1990.

_____ *Against the Barbarians and Other Reflections on Familiar Themes*. University of Missouri Press, 1992.

Broadwater, Jeff. *George Mason: Forgotten Founder*. University of North Carolina Press, 2006.

Burlingame, Michael. *Abraham Lincoln: A Life*, 2 vols. Johns Hopkins University Press, 2008.

Calhoun, John C. *The Papers of John C. Calhoun*. University of South Carolina Press, 2001.

Carwardine, Richard. *Lincoln: A Life of Purpose and Power*. Alfred A. Knopf, 2006.

Catton, Bruce. *The Coming Fury*. Doubleday, 1961.

Craven, Avery. *American Historians and the Civil War*. University of Chicago Press, 1964.,

Crawford, Samuel Wiley. *The Genesis of the Civil War: The Story of Sumter, 1860-61*. Hardpress Publishing, 2012.

Current, Richard N. *The Lincoln Nobody Knows*. McGraw Hill, 1958.

DeCrissey, Elwell. *Lincoln's Lost Speech: The Pivot of His Career.* Hawthorn Books, 1967.

Davis, Jefferson. *The Papers of Jefferson Davis.* Louisiana State University Press, 1992.

DiLorenzo, Thomas J. *The Real Lincoln: A New Look at Abraham Lincoln, His Agenda, and an Unnecessary War.* Three Rivers Press, 2002.

Donald, David Herbert. *Lincoln.* Simon & Schuster, 1995.

Fogel, Robert and Engerman, Stanley. *Time on the Cross: The Economics of American Negro Slavery.* Norton, 1974.

Gara, Larry. *The Liberty Line: The Legend of the Underground Railroad.* University of Kentucky Press, 1967.

Hamilton, Alexander. *The Federalist Papers.* Arlington House, 1966.

Harris, William C. *Lincoln's Rise to the Presidency.* University Press of Kansas, 2007.

Herndon, William and Weik, Jesse M. *Herndon's Life of Lincoln: The History and Recollections of Abraham Lincoln.* Albert & Charles Boni, 1930.

Hertz, Emmanuel, ed. *The Hidden Lincoln: From the Letters and Papers of William H. Herndon.* The Viking Press, 1938.

Jaffa, Harry V. *Crisis of the House Divided: An Interpretation of the Issues in the Lincoln-Douglas Debates.* University of Chicago Press, 1999.

Johnson, Paul. *A History of the American People.* HarperCollins, 1998.

Kendall, Willmore and Carey, George. *The Basic Symbols of the American Political Tradition.* CUA Press, 1970.

Lamon, Ward Hill. *Recollections of Abraham Lincoln, 1847-1865*, Dorothy Lamon, ed. Kessinger Publishing, 2010.

Landess, Thomas H. *Life, Literature, and Lincoln.* Chronicles Press, 2015.

Lincoln, Abraham. *A Documentary Portrait Through His Speeches and Writings.* Don E. Fehrenbacher, ed. Stanford University Press, 1964.

_____ *Speeches and Writings.* 2 vols. Don E. Fehrenbacher, ed. The Library of America, 1989.

Luthin, Reinhard H. *The Real Abraham Lincoln.* Prentice-Hall, 1960.

Masters, Edgar Lee. *Lincoln the Man.* Dodd Mead & Co., 1931.

McPherson, James M. *Abraham Lincoln and the Second American Revolution.* Oxford University Press, 1990.

Minor, Charles L.C. *The Real Lincoln: From the Testimony of His Contemporaries.* Richmond: Everett Waddy Co., 1904.

Nicolay, John G. and Hay, John. *Abraham Lincoln: A History.* The Century Co, 1890.

Randall, James G. *Lincoln the President: Springfield to Gettysburg.* Dodd, Mead & Co., 1945.

Sandburg, Carl. *Abraham Lincoln: The Prairie Years.* Harcourt Brace & World, 1926.

Strode, Hudson. *Jefferson Davis: Southern Patriot, 1808-1860.* Harcourt Brace, 1955.

_____ *Jefferson Davis: Confederate President, 1861-1865.* Harcourt Brace, 1959.

Taylor, John M. *William Henry Seward: Lincoln's Right Hand.* HarperCollins, 1991.

Van Duesen, Glyndon G. *William Henry Seward.* Oxford University Press, 1967.

Wills, Garry. *Lincoln at Gettysburg: The Words that Remade America.* Simon and Schuster, 1992.

Wilson, Douglas L., ed. *The Lincoln Enigma: The Changing Faces of an American Icon.* Oxford University Press, 2001.

Wilson, Douglas L. and Davis, Rodney O. *Herndon's Informants: Letters, Interviews, and Statements about Abraham Lincoln.* University of Illinois Press, 1998.

Wilson, Edmund. *Patriotic Gore: Studies in the Literature of the Civil War.* Oxford University Press, 1962.

Index

Abolitionists, 28, 49, 50-54, 106, 116, 122, 132, 136, 138-139, 163, 171, 178, 191, 197, 220
Adams, Charles Francis, 104
Adams, John Quincy, 18, 24-25, 27, 52, 104-105, 107, 121, 131, 179
American Revolution, 11, 26, 53, 143, 217, 227
Anderson, Robert, 195, 199-201, 204, 206-208, 211
Baker, Edward D., 83-84, 88, 90, 100
Baldwin, John B., 203-204
Banks, 44, 61-62
Beauregard, P.G.T., 205-208
Bible, xi, 12, 15-17, 87, 90, 117-119, 189
Black Hawk War, 30-31
Bledsoe, Albert Taylor, 79

Bloomington speech, 141, 145-146, 174, 194
Breckinridge, John C., 174, 177-178
Brown, John, 136, 171, 183
Browning, Orville, 42, 60, 153
Buchanan, James, 125, 128, 131, 149-151, 153-156, 158, 160, 194-195, 199
Calhoun, John C., 25, 40, 59, 94, 109, 123-124, 133, 168, 171, 193, 225
Cambridge, Mass., speech, 106-107
Campbell, John A., 201
Cass, Lewis, 101, 108, 110, 123
Channing, William Ellery, 117-118, 136
Charleston, S.C., 91, 174, 194-195, 199, 200-202, 204-206, 210-212, 221
Chew, R.S., 204

Chicago, Ill., 90, 94, 108, 114, 118, 133, 151, 161, 165, 174
Christian, xi, 4, 9, 34, 62, 86, 117, 137
Churches, 60, 70, 117, 163
Clary's Grove Boys, 22, 39
Clay, Henry, xi, 18, 19, 24, 28, 31, 37, 65, 85, 92, 101, 103, 110, 123-124, 153, 171
Clinton, De Witt, 43
Colonization, 25, 153
Columbia, S.C., 216
Compromise of 1850, 116, 122, 127
Cooper Union speech, 171-172, 181
Crittenden compromise, 184-185, 193
Dabney, Robert L., 203-204
Davis, David, xi, 114
Davis, Jefferson, 8, 84, 116, 123, 127, 172, 180-182, 185-186, 193, 207

229

Debt, 26, 32, 34-35, 38-39, 42, 57, 61, 62-63, 70, 73, 93, 194
Declaration of Independence, 15, 53, 133-134, 152, 162, 165, 219, 221
Democratic-Republican party, 131
Depression, 41-42, 61, 67, 70-71, 73, 75
Douglas, Stephen A., 42, 44, 58-60, 66-67, 73, 93, 112, 123-128, 131-134, 136-138, 140, 142, 151-152, 155-158, 160-162, 165-170, 172, 174-178, 185, 190, 193, 213
Dred Scott decision, 151, 154, 161-162, 165
Duel, 14, 46, 79-80
Edwards, Ninian, 42, 65, 71
Emancipating slaves, 55, 177
Enslaving free men, 177
Everett, Edward, 175
Fillmore, Millard, 70, 108, 124-125, 150
First inaugural, 186, 189, 194

First shot, 196, 208-209
Fort Sumter, xii, 109, 112, 190, 194-197, 199-202, 204-205, 207-208, 210, 212, 217
Fox, Gustavus V., 30, 199-200, 204, 207-210
Francis, Simeon, 79
Free Soil party, 104, 105, 123, 151
Freeport debate, 168
Fremont, John C., 149-150, 170
Fugitive Slave Law, 116, 121-122
German immigrants, 128, 134-135, 156, 158, 218
Gettysburg Address, 1, 53
Giddings, Joshua R., 93, 122
Graham, William Mentor, 16, 23, 34
Greeley, Horace, 91, 156, 185
Hamilton, Alexander, 179
Hanks, Dennis, 17, 173
Hanks, John, 19, 21
Hanks, Nancy, 11, 21
Hardin, John J., 66, 83-84, 88-90, 100
Harrison, William Henry, 41, 64, 66-67, 69-70, 103, 173

Hay, John, 8, 153, 211
Henry, Dr. Anson, 71
Herndon, William H., xi, 6-7, 14, 32, 85-87, 98-99, 111-113, 117, 126, 146, 150
Honest Abe, xv, 86, 160
House divided, 83, 87, 159-162
Illinois State Bank, 78
Internal improvements, 18-19, 25-27, 30-31, 37-38, 41-43, 45-47, 62, 64, 66, 70, 73, 78, 89, 91, 94-95, 104-107, 116
irrepressible conflict, 169
Jackson, Andrew, 18-19, 24, 31, 33-34, 37, 44, 58, 67, 104, 123, 125, 156, 171
Jefferson, Thomas, xii, 24, 105, 107, 124, 131, 139, 153
Johnson, Andrew, 185
Johnston, Sarah, 12
Kansas, 126-127, 132-133, 135-136, 138, 142-144, 154-155, 157, 160
Kansas-Nebraska Bill, 122, 140, 155

Know-Nothing party, 125, 128, 139-140, 150
Koerner, Gustave, 158
Lamon, Ward, xi, 200-202
Lecompton Constitution, 154, 157
Lee, Robert E., 8
Levering, Mercy Ann, 69, 74
Lexington, Ky., 65-66, 92, 113
Liberty Party, 85
Lincoln, Edward, 88, 117
Lincoln, Mary Todd, xi, 65-68, 70-71, 73-77, 79-81, 100, 155, 174
Lincoln, Robert Todd, 77
Lincoln, Sarah, 13
Lincoln, Thomas, 11-13, 16, 18, 24, 58, 119
Lincoln, William Wallace, 114
Logan, Stephen T., 6, 66, 74, 77, 85, 86
Long Nine, 42-43, 46-47, 57, 65
Long, Alexander, 212, 213
Lyceum Address, 53, 54, 118
Malice toward none, 4
Marx, Karl, 180, 183

Marxist/Marxism, viii, xi, 117
Mason, George, 32, 132
Masters, Edgar Lee, x
Matheny, James, 90, 117
Mexican War, 84-85, 94-95, 97-100, 108, 111, 124, 149, 216
Missouri Compromise, 116, 127, 140, 144, 150-151, 184
Morrill, Lot M., 222
Negroes, 17, 21, 28, 40, 50, 109, 121, 131, 134-135, 139, 143, 152, 160, 165, 191
New England, ix, xii, 15, 18, 26, 50, 103-104, 106, 117, 125, 136, 169, 171, 237
New Salem, Ill., 5, 16, 22-23, 29-35, 38-39, 47
Nicolay, John G., 8, 153, 211
Nullification, 33, 225, 237
Owens, Mary, 40, 42, 60
Paine, Tom, 34
Parker, Theodore, 117, 136
Peter Cartwright, 84, 90
Phillips, Wendell, 223

Pickens, Francis W., 200-201, 204-206
Pierce, Franklin, 124-127, 158, 160, 181
Popular sovereignty, 127, 133, 136, 140, 151, 154, 168, 172
Protectionism, xi, 9, 18
Railroads, 43, 46, 106, 114, 216
Railsplitter, 5
River and Harbor Convention, 90
Rutledge, Ann, 23, 81
Scott, Winfield, 124
Secession, 33, 79, 99, 116, 145, 172, 178-183, 185-186, 189, 191, 195, 196, 200, 204, 219
Seward, William H., 8, 103, 106, 107, 108, 123, 128, 169, 170-171, 174, 186, 199, 201-203, 207
Seymour, Horatio, 185
Sherman, William T., 216-217
Shields, James, 78-80, 88
Simeon Francis, 58, 67, 79
Slavery, ix, xii, 3, 8, 15, 18, 21, 25, 49, 50-53, 65, 75, 79, 85-86, 93-94, 100, 103, 105-109, 112, 116-117, 121, 124,

127-128, 133-134, 136, 138-140, 142-145, 149-152, 154-155, 157, 159-160, 162-163, 165, 168-169, 172, 179, 181-184, 191, 219-220
  In District of Columbia, 50, 68, 93-94, 109, 116, 184
Speed, Joshua, 5, 34, 43, 57, 62, 74-76, 86, 88, 90, 112
Springfield, Ill., xi, 21-23, 29, 38-39, 42, 44-47, 52-53, 57, 59-60, 63-66, 70-71, 74-76, 90, 97, 101, 108, 113, 124, 133, 140, 159, 177, 186
Stanton, Edwin M., 114
Stephens, Alexander H., 100, 180, 185
Stuart, John Todd, 34, 37-38, 47, 57, 59, 66, 71, 73-74, 86, 90
Swett, Leonard, 7
Taney, Roger B., 151, 158, 160
Tariff, 18, 25, 27, 31, 66, 78, 89, 91, 94-96, 105, 152-153, 158, 191, 196, 204
Taylor, Zachary, 70, 100-101, 103, 108, 110-111, 118, 123-125, 170-171
Todd, Robert, 65, 88, 113
Trumbull, Lyman, 135, 170, 182
Tyler, John, 66, 103, 125, 185
Uriah Heep, 165
Van Buren, Martin, 41, 67-70, 75-76, 89, 95, 104-105, 123, 125, 132, 156, 184
Vandalia, Ill., 38, 41, 43, 45-47
Volney, Comte de, 34
Wade, Benjamin F., 122
Washington, George, xii, 1-4, 16
Webster, Daniel, 41, 94, 103, 123-124, 171
Weed, Thurlow, 91, 108
Welles, Gideon, 202
Whitney, Henry C., 142, 144-146, 174
Wilmot Proviso, 95

ABOUT THE AUTHOR

DR. CHARLES T. PACE was born and raised in Greenville, N.C. After his undergraduate studies at the University of North Carolina at Chapel Hill, he completed medical school at Jefferson Medical College in Philadelphia and his residency in ophthalmology at the University of Virginia School of Medicine. He served as a flight surgeon in the United States Air Force. Dr. Pace practiced medicine in Greenville for over 50 years before his retirement. His interest in Southern history and culture has been lifelong. Dr. Pace is the author of the first book published by Shotwell Publishing, *Southern Independence. Why War?*

AVAILABLE FROM SHOTWELL

JOYCE BENNETT

Maryland, My Maryland: The Cultural Cleansing of a Small Southern State

JERRY BREWER

Dismantling the Republic

ANDREW P. CALHOUN, JR.

My Own Darling Wife: Letters From a Confederate Volunteer [John Francis Calhoun]

JOHN CHODES

Segregation: Federal Policy or Racism?

Washington's KKK: The Union League During Southern Reconstruction

PAUL C. GRAHAM

Confederaphobia: An American Epidemic

When the Yankees Come: Former South Carolina Slaves Remember Sherman's Invasion

JAMES R. KENNEDY

Dixie Rising: Rules for Rebels

JAMES R. & WALTER D. KENNEDY

Punished with Poverty: The Suffering South

PHILIP LEIGH

The Devil's Town: Hot Spring During the Gangster Era

MICHAEL MARTIN

Southern Grit: Sensing the Siege at Petersburg

CHARLES T. PACE

Southern Independence. Why War?

JAMES RUTLEDGE ROESCH

From Founding Fathers to Fire Eaters: The Constitutional Doctrine of States' Rights in the Old South

KIRKPATRICK SALE

Emancipation Hell: The Tragedy Wrought By Lincoln's Emancipation Proclamation

KAREN STOKES

A Legion of Devils: Sherman in South Carolina

Carolina Love Letters

JOHN VINSON

Southerner, Take Your Stand!

CLYDE N. WILSON

Lies My Teacher Told Me: The True History of the War for Southern Independence

SOUTHERN READER'S GUIDE

The Old South: 50 Essential Books (I)

THE WILSON FILES

The Yankee Problem: An American Dilemma (1)

Nullification: Reclaiming Consent of the Governed (2)

Annals of the Stupid Party: Republicans Before Trump (3)

GREEN ALTAR BOOKS (LITERARY IMPRINT)

RANDALL IVEY

A New England Romance & Other SOUTHERN Stories

JAMES EVERETT KIBLER

Tiller (Clay Bank County, IV)

Lincoln As He Really Was

Karen Stokes
- *Belles: A Carolina Romance*
- *Honor in the Dust*
- *The Immortals*
- *The Soldier's Ghost: A Tale of Charleston*

Gold-Bug (Mystery & Suspense Imprint)

Michael Andrew Grissom
- *Billie Jo*

Brandi Perry
- *Splintered: A New Orleans Tale*

Martin L. Wilson
- *To Jekyll and Hide*

Publisher's Note

IF YOU ENJOYED THIS BOOK or found it useful, interesting, or informative, we'd be very grateful if you would post a brief review of it on the retailer's website or your social media feed.

In the current political and cultural climate, it is important that we get accurate, Southern-friendly material into the hands of our friends and neighbours. *Your support can really make a difference* in helping us unapologetically celebrate and defend our Southern heritage, culture, history, and home!

FREE BOOK OFFER

SIGN-UP FOR NEW RELEASE NOTIFICATIONS and receive a FREE DOWNLOADABLE EDITION of *Lies My Teacher Told Me: The True History of the War for Southern Independence* by Dr. Clyde N. Wilson by visiting FreeLiesBook.com or by texting the word "Dixie" to 345345. You can always unsubscribe and keep the book, so you've got nothing to lose!

Southern without Apology

www.ingramcontent.com/pod-product-compliance
Lightning Source LLC
Chambersburg PA
CBHW050549160426
43199CB00015B/2594